CHRISTIAN ORTHODOXY REVISITED

CHRISTIAN ORTHODOXY REVISITED

The challenge of catholic renewal today

MICHAEL MARSHALL

MOREHOUSE BARLOW

Wilton

Center for Biblical Studies
514-3777

Dedicated to my mother

First American Edition 1985 by
Morehouse Barlow Co., Inc.
78 Danbury Road
Wilton, Connecticut 06897

ISBN 8192-1357-8

Library of Congress Catalog Card Number 84-62322

Printed in the United States of America

First published in Great Britain in 1978 as *Glory Under
Your Feet* by Darton, Longman and Todd LTD, 89 Lillie
Road, London SW6—1UD.

CONTENTS

PREFACE TO THE AMERICAN EDITION

If a statement were entirely new, it would be unintelligible. To be intelligible, to make sense, requires that what we say be in continuity with past perceptions, thoughts, and language. To the neophyliac mind, the admission that something is not entirely new is fatal. . . . I am persuaded, however, that bringing together what we know or think we know is both challenging and important. It is in examining the taken-for-granted truths that our errors are unearthed.

Richard John Neuhaus, *The Naked Public Square* Published by William B. Eerdmans Publishing Company 1984 Page 4

So I shall doubtless disappoint the neophyliacs by cooperating with Morehouse Barlow in reprinting my very first book, published as long ago in England as 1978 by Darton, Longman and Todd under the English title of *Glory Under Your Feet*. Nevertheless, I also am persuaded on arriving in America for a new chapter of ministry, that if we wish to be intelligible there must indeed be a strong and substantial measure of "continuity with past perceptions, thoughts and language." So much which has paraded as renewal in the life of the Christian churches has failed to understand precisely this point and has fragmented into trivial contemporary enthusiasms, destined to be shortlived and to disillusion their disciples. Furthermore, such a view of renewal will almost certainly give way to an equally distorted concept of the way forward through the very opposite of renewal—namely, a movement of reaction. All error has that strange power to create double confusion: we do not go back to the problem and see the naked need to get the right answer this time; our motivation is already blinded by the need to get a *different* answer the next time at all costs. So, therefore, renewal wrongly understood will always herald a time and a season of reaction. Since the renewal movements of the seventies, there is ample evidence—not least in the climate of American religion—of strong forces of reaction brought nearer and more persistently into the public and political life of our society by the ongoing religious revival (prophesied in that earlier edition of my book) which shows no sign of abating. It is no accident that in the presidential election in America in 1984, the place of religion in politics reached a crescendo of more decibels that in any political campaign in modern history, and some of the horror stories of religious revival to which I alluded in the opening chapter of *Glory Under Your Feet* written in 1978 have not in any way lost their ring of contemporary significance in the decade of the eighties.

For frankly, even the very word renewal is already a jaded word. That is not to say that the breath of renewal through the life of the Holy Spirit is not a great blessing to all who receive it and also that the need for continuous renewal both individually and corporately is a perennial prerequisite in the life of the Christian church if it is to be in any real sense a church which can persuade men and women to make a costly and lively act of faith in Jesus Christ afresh in each successive generation. Yet it is surprising (or perhaps not quite so surprising) to observe how renewal (necessarily so elusive and irregimented) in its springtime soon, like the cuckoo, goes flat with the onset of summer and rapidly degenerates into yet another "religious movement" as the seasons pass by. I've even visited dioceses where committees for renewal have been formed, predictably issuing reports and reviews, setting this latest idol up as a thing-in-itself, for which even budgetary provision is soon unapologetically demanded!

Yet this perversion of renewal persists for at least two reasons. In the first place, not unlike the cuckoo, it has a distinctive tone to it: it looks and it sounds like real religion— and moreover like that sort of religion which makes a difference and which is not ashamed to be called and to appear religious. Above all else it appears to be a religion which works. It is evocative of past "ages of faith" and rapidly affects a weariness with the niceties of debate, with intellectual challenges to faith, claiming an urgency and a naivete and an effectiveness which will and indeed does readily equip people to withstand the alien and secular forces of the age. In a word false renewal in one generation will be the best breeding ground for the fundamentalism of a decade or so later and furthermore that very fundamentalism writ large will (again not unlike the cuckoo) grow fat and soon displace all other alternatives from the nest.

And all this at a time when the mainstream churches persist in conducting debate in place of mission, evaluation in place of evangelism. Sitting on bean bags, they try to look as much as possible like sensible and concerned (those two very dangerous words) inhabitants of a matter-of-fact world of faith which refuses to make any demands upon the imagination, the world of fantasy, and the supernatural, or to draw upon many aspects of traditional Christian beliefs. I remember, only shortly after arriving in America, attending a meeting of clergy and listening to a learned dissertation from an Oxford don on the history of biblical criticism. For me, and I am sure for many of my colleagues, it was a scholarly and helpful review of biblical criticism from the nineteenth century until the present day. Its overriding assessment was aimed at analysing just how much or how little (especially in the light of Bultmann and the German critics) we could still attribute to the life and sayings of Jesus Christ. But the sadness to me was not so much that clergy should be compelled to give precious time to this interesting though largely academic exercise, but rather how very out of date the whole lecture was in assessing the climate of belief in America in the eighties—and not least in the South, the bible-belt, and in areas where renewal, revival and fundamentalism were probably reaching a new peak of intensity. A Martian would have assessed the situation more accurately. For fundamentalism, credulity and the willingness to believe *anything* and *everything* were surely the problems to which messengers of the gospel in the eighties in America needed to address themselves, rather than to replay the weary disc of the reductionism of the fifties, which, I suspect, had been the background to which our lecturer had originally addressed his words, when they had first been uttered in their original form. He had failed, I believe, to follow through the shape of things from the reductionism and rationalism of the mainstream churches in the fifties to renewal and from renewal to reaction and fundamentalism which is very much the scene of American religion and the religion in the west of the eighties.

But, there is a second front on which these religious movements and the mainstream churches have failed to connect. For surely it was the liberals of the mainstream churches who in the fifties and again in the seventies rightly demanded a relationship between religious committment and political debate. Admittedly in a very predictable and left wing direction, the religion-and-politics champions had held the platform and both liberal protestantism and the liberal catholicism of Vatican II came out strongly in a unanimous voice with a program of political and moral issues ranging all the way from feminism to nuclear disarmament and from human rights to liberation theology. For the renewal movements, especially among charismatics in their springtime—and especially in South Africa when I visited the church there in the early seventies—refused to have anything to do with politics and certainly in the early days seemed to preach a religion which addressed itself primarily, if not exclusively, to personal experience and personal salvation.

However, a very different day has dawned in the mid eighties. For in a different way, with totally different results, the reaction to renewal of fundamentalism is the religion of the new right. For two can play at religion and politics, and the issue as it emerged in the presidential campaign of 1984 made the liberal left wing humanitarianism of the earlier decades look not only jaded and tired, but strangely "irreligious" and even conservative and preservationist. For this new right wing religious declaration seems to address itself in an almost strangely radical way to the era of apocalyptic radicalism—recalling unashamedly much of the atmosphere and the Church of the New Testament. For such insights are strongly fired with the approach of the second millennium and the disciples of this latest wave of religion-and-politics are not ashamed to recall Christians to the inevitability of the end of all things (either by human willfulness in a nuclear holocaust or by divine intervention). To such people it seems to make little difference for they are convinced that both will be agonizing and have about them a note of finality and irrevocability. As the second millennium neurosis increases, the disciples of such movements are hardly surprisingly growing in numbers and in their impact. Here's a state of things!

At such a time—and we have been this way many times in history—there is "a yet more excellent way" which refuses either to espouse the citadel mentality around the so-called certainties of the past, or on the other hand to cut off its head in the name of revolution. It is the way by which man himself has emerged as recognizable as a species yet as adaptable in changing environments. It is the way of evolution which is never ashamed to rehearse again and again the story of its development in such a way that the past can actually nurture and feed the present, so that in its turn, it will be sufficiently robust in its response to its contemporary environment that it does not need either to react or to revolt but genuinely to evolve into a true and sturdy future. It is of course the way of the "wise scribe" commended in the New Testament by Jesus who is not ashamed to bring out of his store both things old as well as things new.

For such a process to flourish in a way which is creative and which feeds and sustains faith the story must be told again and again. "Tell me the old, old story"—that is always the challenge of the church in every new situation. When a civilization or a culture forgets its stories it loses its direction. The stories of the Christian faith are more than the bare bones of dogma. They are lively stories clothed with human flesh and blood experience. They have refrains which are not ashamed even to be set to music and frequently it is to the music of marching, for it is the collective experience through song and story of a people who are essentially a people on the move—pilgrim people who have always tended to sing as they march. Many of their songs and many of their stories take their listeners down "memory lane" and evoke a past which seems to refuse to let go of them and clings to them in such a way that the present events of contemporary life have about them a new richness and depth. Such is the nature of Christian orthodoxy. It is not the mere scaffolding of credal statements. It consists of stories of experiences and is indeed a living picture gallery of the faces of men and women who have tested the truths of faith in life and have vindicated those truths in the crucible of costly experience thoughout human history.

This is the territory which we need to visit and revisit frequently. In short, it is the faith and life of the church—a church which is catholic, apostolic and holy and which is "at one" with its Author and with all who are in some way part of the divine drama.

Such a gospel will be a rich gospel because it will not be limited by relevancy, by the need to be contemporary and certainly not by that most bedevilling temptation of wanting to appear to be something new. It will be a gospel which will not fit *into* any one age because it is a gospel which is not *of* any age. It is ageless, it is eternal and therefore eternally relevant: "The whole gospel, addressed to the whole man for the whole world." Originally, I discovered that phrase from a Baptist who interviewed me on my first television talk-show in America. However, as I was quick to point out to my Baptist friend, such a slogan might well be adopted by every Christian (of many denominations) who is ready to recite the outlines of his religion and faith in the words of the creed when he claims to believe "in one holy catholic and apostolic church." Of course the result will not be easy answers to all the contemporary questions which rightly beset the church in our own age. A firm faith for tough times must not rest on the plinth of idolatry. The creeds of the church, the teaching of scripture and the insights of human reason and experience (and all three of these are elements in the stories to which I have referred) do not end up with neat and tidy answers. They are not intended to do so. They are intended to be the tools which help each generation to do the work of faith and they are intended to equip each generation with precisely those tools which can begin to forge answers to difficult and thorny questions. So orthodoxy (or right belief) like good health is not so much something you can sell, acquire, keep or lose. It is a condition, which is probably so elusive that (like joy) we lose it the very moment we think we can pin it down and the moment we begin to be self-conscious about it. Yet this faith and church of which Christians have spoken with enthusiasm over the ages and which they have called orthodoxy is neither so elusive that we should not set out, determined to sell all until we can find it; nor is it so sophisticated and remote that the Christian life ends up by becoming little more than a long and meaningless search in a desert of doubt and unbelief. It is perhaps best described as a gift which needs unwrapping. Part of the delight both of the giver and of the receiver is not to cut short that very process of unwrapping: on the contrary, part of the wonder and the thankfulness grows as each layer is unravelled and at each new revelation and insight locked within the parcel and its attractive many layers of decorative wrapping.

So, "faith of our fathers" is not the slogan which is intended to cut short all discussion and silence all critics. But it is a faith which needs to be known, researched, rehearsed and represented. Most people who have rejected orthodox Christianity have done so because they have largely been ignorant of it. I believe therefore that at a time of fragmentation and reaction such as is the climate in the American religious scene today, there is a fresh and urgent need for the reaffirmation of orthodoxy. Christians will not discover their identity in isolation from the past. We discover our identity by *identifying* with others who have about them precisely the features which we recognise, whose words we need to incorporate into our own rather limited vocabulary and expression and above all whose experiences in Christian faith and life have driven them beyond all words. In short we can become saints best when we identify with the saints as surely as fans identify with their heroes and are ready to follow them wherever they go.

For in fact you cannot be a Christian in isolation: either in isolation from other Christians around you or from other Christians who have gone before you. A contemporary Christian is in that sense a contradiction in terms. So this book is offered unashamedly for a seond time: it is the household of faith revisited not in order that we might blow up the drawbridge, shut down the portcullis and turn the household into a bastion or citadel with walls which separate those within it from those who are outside it. That is certainly not the Christian view of orthodoxy. Rather it is much more something like a family reunion: knowing where I belong before I can know where my longings might take me; knowing where I am at home before I can be truly free to explore new territory and above all knowing where I can return and where I will be welcome even when I have got it wrong; that is what I think the Christian means by the household of faith. "It is in examining the taken for granted truths that our errors are unearthed." Home is the only place where I can afford to take others for granted and where errror will come to light best because I no longer need to be on the defensive. Home and family are where I can also be taken for granted and for what I am neither more nor less—namely, a forgiven sinner and therefore an unfinished saint in the making.

So the household of faith revisited is really the best place on earth to have the family rows. It is the place where the young are not allowed to be too self-conscious and yet where the old and the silent are never allowed to be forgotten. In a word it is hard to know if there is anywhere else on earth where you really can grow up and evolve without either being spoiled, overprotected or just lost in oblivion.

For the Church at its best was God's gift to us and is intended by Him to be such a household. At times in history of course it has been overprotective, claustrophobic, exclusive and destructive of growth and development. To say that is to reinforce the well-known fact that there can be bad families and bad houses, not to dispense with the family or to pretend that we should despise home. Furthermore, Christians believe that our real home and our real family ultimately are in heaven and that it is that fact which gives to our earthly homes and families their real flavor and warmth. But in the meantime, Christians on earth really do need the household of faith. They need to know it, love it and visit it and revisit it frequently. The following pages belong to such a visit and hopefully invite and encourage the church to be truly and continuously renewed around its own true and lasting identity in such a way that we shall be truly recognizable not with a past or bogus religiosity. Rather, we will be men and women who have frequently "been with Jesus," eaten and drunk at his table with that proper familiarity that those first disciples experienced: a familiarity which soon became an expulsive affection, ruthlessly driving them out with a message which was indeed to become "the whole gospel, addressed to the whole man for the whole world."

+ Michael Marshall
Episcopal Director,
Anglican Institute,
St. Louis, Missouri

Thanksgiving Day 1984

PREFACE

Much of this book is simply a personal affirmation of my own faith at those moments when that faith is bright and strong. Of course there are other moments, as for everyone, when faith seems remote and even alien. In those strong moments, however, Christian orthodoxy or main stream Christianity, seems to me to have a strange and elusive power of being just that bit more relevant, somewhat more profound and even, if I dare say so, more beautiful than the other intellectual possibilities with which it has always been in conflict. I am not pretending that what I have chosen to call catholic Christianity is a clearly defined body of teaching with clean-cut edges: that is evidently not the case. Nevertheless, there is a wealth of teaching and Christian experience which forms the main stream of Christianity over 2,000 years and it is to that living stream that I am led back and back again, discovering it to be living water, and the best of all other possible alternatives – alternatives which I have frequently considered and even helped to revive and popularise.

For in many ways I think I could invent another sort of Christianity which at first sight would fit more comfortably and more immediately into the mould of my own prejudiced thinking and the particular thought-forms of this generation. I have done it many times, certainly in my own life, sometimes just for self-satisfaction, or at other times in order to score a point or to win a case. But, at the end of the day, it has failed to have that inner ring of truth and that gracious and generous authority which alone can satisfy. So in many ways these pages are the personal record of a Christian orthodoxy 'revisited'. For it is this strange power of Christianity to renew itself when the structures to which it has been wedded and through which it has felicitously expressed itself have crumbled, that is the mark and test of catholic Christianity continually vindicating itself in moments of resurrection and new life.

I hope I do not give the impression that in matters of faith there is a short cut, and much of what I have written with such confidence may even offend or bruise those for whom faith has been a painful struggle. 'We may not be taken up and transported to our journey's end but must travel thither on foot, traversing the whole distance of the narrow way' (Clement of Alexandria). But unlike the slick travel agent, may I in these pages resemble rather an enthusiastic tourist by sharing my enthusiasm about a journey and some geography which may be in danger of being disregarded by its dated packaging and yet which is, I believe, still a 'yet more excellent way'.

Of course Christianity has had a bad history and much that it has claimed and done is unworthy of its commission and of its author. To say that is to say little more than to affirm its human form—warts and all. It is equally true, however, to endorse this other ingredient of renewal at moments when all seems lost and dead—a renewal which is a living vindication of the other side of Christianity, namely its truly supernatural and glorious origins. The Church ought to have died long ago on any normal historical prognosis, either when the Middle Ages crumbled or when other social and economic structures had 'had their little day'. But here it is, being renewed and reformed afresh and sturdily refusing to 'lie down'! Yet that renewal is not to be found merely in updating the packaging, but rather by digging deep into a living tradition and bringing out of that treasure 'things new and old'. So, it is perhaps more in the spirit of a treasure hunt that I offer these pages in which my life and my work and my faith already daily involve me. For the failure of the Church is not the last word that has to be said about it; there is another word and another promise from the one who is not only the author but also the perfector of our faith and it is the word of a renewal which is more than mere innovation and of a victory which is not simply a new triumphalism.

History and my personal failure as a Christian disciple daily remind me that, of course, the Church

> grew so far, almost at once, from anything which can have been intended, and became so blood-stained and persecuting and cruel and warlike, and made small and trivial things so important, and tried to exclude everything not done in a certain way and by certain people, and stamped out heresies with such cruelty and rage. And this failure of the Christian church, of every branch of it in every country, is one of the saddest things that has happened in all the world. But it is what happens when a magnificent idea has to be worked out by human beings who do not understand much of it but interpret it in their own way and think they are guided by God, whom they have not yet grasped. And yet they have grasped something, so that the church has always had great magnificence and much courage ... and it has flowered up in learning and culture and beauty and art, to set against its darkness and incivility and obscurantism and barbarity and nonsense, and it has produced saints and martyrs and kindness and goodness, though these have also occurred freely outside it, and it is a wonderful and most extraordinary pageant of contradictions, and I, at least, want to be inside it, though it is foolishness to most of my friends. (*Towers of Trebizond*: Rose Macaulay)

It is precisely that 'wonderful and most extraordinary pageant of contradictions' which fascinates me most and which will not let me go, and which, I believe, should be the point of departure in all our explorations into God.

*   *   *

The author of a book is often a member of a team, the names of whom are largely buried in the unconscious memories of previous teachers, saintly examples and patient guides. That is inevitable. But equally there are members of that team who have so obviously and evidently made possible the finished object. Among these I should like to name particularly Miss Mary Baddeley who in record time typed the script, Dr Eric Mascall who saw the first draft and helped by encouragement and correction, and not least Robin Baird-Smith without whose patience the whole enterprise would never have been possible. The Revd. Peter Strange kindly corrected the proofs. To them all my deep gratitude.

INTRODUCTORY CHAPTER

THE CONTEMPORARY RELIGIOUS CLIMATE

The reaction of the seventies

'We are heading into a profoundly religious age,' wrote McLuhan in 1968. At the time that he wrote this, it must have seemed the ultimate contradiction of the most obvious and immediate evidence, especially to those who had grown up in the balmy days of the post-Second-World-War affluent society. The fifties had been a period of the apparent triumph of rationalist technology with a brash and convincing confidence in the success of a largely materialistic world, when many seemed certain that we had 'never had it so good' and that this would continue at least for the foreseeable future. In such a world, religion, the supernatural and the mystical held little interest for the Western mind—a mind obsessed with the concrete world of its own making, the political struggles between Western and Eastern ideologies, when politicians were still heroes and space travellers heralds of the new age of scientific and technological triumphalism.

In such a world, if religion in any form—and not least in its Christian form—were to survive the century, it seemed obvious that it would require the skilful work of Ockham's razor in a further and ruthless reductionism which would dispose of the increasing embarrassment of prayer and meditation, the miraculous and the supernatural, in favour of a gospel of matter-of-fact activist social con-

cern, without distinctive creeds and with no appetite for transcendent experience. This movement in reductionism was yet a further
stage of a previous movement of liberal protestantism so gloriously
and penetratingly summarised in the words of Richard Niebuhr:

> The romantic conception of the kingdom of God involved no
> discontinuities, no crises, no tragedies or sacrifices, no loss of all
> things, no cross, and resurrection. In ethics it reconciled the
> interests of the individual with those of society by means of faith
> in a natural identity of interests or in the benevolent, altruistic
> character of man. In politics and economics it slurred over
> national and class divisions, seeing only the growth of unity and
> ignoring the increase of self-assertion and exploitation. In religion
> it reconciled God and man by deifying the latter and humanizing
> the former ... Christ the Redeemer became Jesus the teacher or
> the spiritual genius in whom the religious capacities of mankind
> were fully developed.... Evolution, growth, development, the
> culture of the religious life, the nurture of the kindly sentiments,
> the extension of humanitarian ideals, and the progress of civiliza-
> tion took the place of the Christian revolution.... A God with-
> out wrath brought men without sin into a kingdom without
> judgement through the ministrations of a Christ without a cross.
> (H. Richard Niebuhr *The Kingdom of God in America*)

At the popular level, this movement of reductionism in the fifties and
sixties acquired the umbrella term of the 'death of God' movement
and was summarised in the much misused and largely misunder-
stood slogan borrowed from the prophets of the new religion,
Bonhoeffer and Tillich, 'a religionless Christianity'. 'Man come of
age' no longer would need, nor should he be embarrassed by, the
unnecessary accretions of the past ages of faith, with their myths and
superstitions. The Church of the twentieth century must now face
massive re-appraisal of its creeds and its practices. In theological
colleges and seminaries the climate was wholly against prayer and
chapel disciplines. This climate was a winter of cold rational func-
tionalism, and in the 'death of God movement' the Church was
preparing to bury or burn all that seemed to smack of the excessive

and unnecessary in the concrete and commonsense landscape of the secular city.

'The man who marries the spirit of the age will be a widower in the next,' wrote Dean Inge. During the sixties there was a sudden and massive reaction, largely rooted in the younger generation, against the confident, technological materialism of the previous age. 'Everything to live with, and nothing to live for' might well have been the epitaph on the tomb of the fifties, as more and more young people in the sixties, frequently from 'good schools' and well-heeled families dropped out of the rat-race of 'educationalism' with the *cursus honorum* of school and university, refusing the all-too-categorised strait-jackets of a functional society, and opting for what on reflection we might well call the 'secular mysticism' of the sixties. This movement represented a rejection of the establishment, the structural and the rational, and sought the immediate and spontaneous experience, ignoring history and indifferent to productivity or success. It was as though many had come to the breaking point in a long headache: we had had enough of the imprisonment within the limitations of purely rational and cerebral disciplines. 'The madman', says Chesterton, 'is not the man who has lost his reason, but rather the man who has lost everything except his reason.'

It was against this long chapter of 'madness', culminating in the post-war affluent society of the fifties, that the secular 'charismatic movement' most strongly reacted. Suddenly there was a curiosity about a whole world of experience outside the rational, a bizarre world of greater intensity and passions, of trips and transcendental experiences, written and sung about by the ever-expanding big business of pop stars in general and the Beatles in particular. The password through the door to this new world of greater perception was love, and the key which opened it in the sixties was the key of the chemically induced trip of drugs or 'smoking'. The Beatles in their lyrics and life spanned the whole of that trip. They represented a strong and popular rejection of the arid rationalism and confident materialism of the fifties. At another level and speaking to a different audience, writers like Laing and Huxley claimed that much mental ill-health was precisely the deprivation and starvation of the total man in the name of the rational man. Here in sophisticated packaging was the gut reaction with its insistence upon a new quest, a new journey, a new trip, without maps, signposts or policemen. Flowers, love and transcendental experiences were the characteristics of this savage reaction against the serpents of politics and the high-priesthood of technology which had enjoyed an unquestioned rule in previous decades.

As the seventies dawned, this reaction against the 'madness' of rationalism took on a new form. It became interested in and obsessed by the spiritual. Techniques of transcendental meditation, Zen and Yoga techniques promised to open the doors of perception without the aid of drugs and chemically induced experiences. The Beatles went to India to learn to meditate! Religion—all except the Christian variety—was once again in vogue; there was a religious revival everywhere except in the churches. The religionless Church of the fifties had given way to the churchless religion of the seventies. (Two could play at that game!) This new obsession with the spiritual, while ignoring the churches, was curious, nevertheless, about the person of Jesus. He was the object of pop songs and musicals, sometimes as hero and sometimes simply as an opportunity for blasphemy and obscenities, as though it seemed necessary to irrigate the collective subconscious taboos of past centuries about the nature of what is holy and unmentionable.

Of course it is not a long jump from this to a revival of a popular and morbid curiosity about the demonic—superstition, sorcery and demonic obsession. Paul Johnson writes: 'Educated people in the West often happily juxtapose in their minds scientific rationalism with crude superstition (eg astrology).'* But the leap is nearer than we might suppose. In an age when technology can land men on the moon and tame the stars, astrology flourishes, the myths of Tolkien are best sellers, and box-office successes are most easily secured with films and plays about the dark side of religion and demons. Religion has once again raised its dangerous and ugly head. We thought in the past that we had put the cat of religion out of the back door in the evening of the fifties, only to be confronted with the tiger of new religions on the following morning of the seventies growling at the

* See Paul Johnson *Enemies of Society* (Weidenfeld and Nicolson 1977).

front door and demanding to be let in. 'You can drive out nature with a pitchfork,' says Horace, 'but she goes on coming back.' So with natural religion—what Andrew Greeley writing in 1973 terms the 'Persistance of Religion'. 'I do not think', he writes, 'religion is in a state of collapse, and none of the empirical data that I have available leads me to see that it is.'

It is not insignificant that many of the prophets and high-priests who reigned supreme in the reductionist theology of the fifties and sixties have had to reverse their prophecies or somewhat change their directions in the light of this new age of 'religion'. Professor Peter Berger in his *Rumour of Angels* wrote in 1969:

> Whatever the situation may have been in the past, *today* the supernatural as a meaningful reality is absent or remote from the horizons of everyday life of large numbers, very probably of the majority, of people in modern societies, who seem to manage to get along without it quite well.

However, in 1977 he wrote in the *Washington Post* a long article on the religious revival which had already hit America and which was strongest in those churches with 'a strong profile' of belief and behaviour. Similarly it is interesting to monitor the titles and content of Harvey Cox's books. In 1965 he wrote his famous *The Secular City—A Christian acclamation of both the emergence of secular urban civilization and the breakdown of traditional religion* (G. B. Hall). The *Feast of Fools*, however, followed in 1969 noting the re-emergence of festivity and fantasy in Western culture and recalling the part it had played in earlier traditions of Christian worship and practice. In 1974 he wrote his book entitled *The Seduction of the Spirit—The use and misuse of people's religion*. This seems a far cry from the unquestioned emergence of secular urban civilisation, and is an interesting commentary on the changing pattern of Western culture from the fifties to the seventies.

The dangers of religion and secular mysticism

At first sight, from a Christian viewpoint, it might seem that the seventies are a better wicket for the churches than the fifties. Surely, we might argue, spiritualism and a curiosity about the unseen, a new interest in meditation and prayer techniques are infinitely preferable as a starting point for any discussion about Christian claims than the blatant materialism and confident rationalism of the fifties. It was Bishop Michael Ramsey who, with characteristic insight and perception, reflected upon his time as Archbishop of Canterbury (1961–74) when he regularly conducted university and college teaching-weeks. In 1961, at the outset of his primacy, all the questions from students were on social concerns and justice, politics and economics and the claims of science against religion, but by the beginning of the seventies the questions were predominantly about prayer and meditation and spiritual things.

I think that if I had to choose a date for the turning point in this reaction, it would be 1969. I had been a chaplain in London University from 1964, and the main thrust of the work in those years was the sustaining of an apologetic for belief in God and commitment to Christ. Then in 1969 I helped in the Oxford University Mission jointly conducted by Bishop Ian Ramsey and Archbishop Anthony Bloom. Bishop Ramsey gave his brilliant lectures in the Sheldonian each evening on the rational basis for belief with a style and content reminiscent of William Temple's great apologetics. But the attendances were not impressive and were not well maintained throughout the mission. On the other hand, Archbishop Anthony Bloom conducted his daily 'School in Prayer' in Exeter College Chapel and the attendances rose dramatically each day until it was impossible to get a seat even on the floor of the ante-chapel to hear addresses which totally by-passed intellectual issues and plunged straight into the experiential and the spiritual. For me that was a significant moment—it marked the end of the tyranny of the rational and the beginning of the seduction of the spiritual and the charismatic.

Of course, it is true that the Christian presentation has never claimed that the mind and the intellect are the whole story. Nevertheless, although the Christian claim would be to a faith which was super-rational it would never align itself to a faith which was blatantly irrational. 'A madman', to use Chesterton's analogy, 'is a sort of head without a body, but a body without a head is a ghost, and there is little to choose between madmen and ghosts.' We were given the double commandment as Christians: to be 'as wise as serpents' and 'as tender as doves'. Our present generation has opted for Jonathan Livingston Seagull, rising above it all in a higher and more spiritual realm. 'I suspect all of us who visit the worlds of Jonathan Seagull will never want to return,' is the blatant admission of one reviewer, which is proudly displayed on the dust jacket of the book. But detachment of this kind has little if anything to do with Christianity, although it may frequently invoke the 'spiritual' as the basis of its conviction and action. Weariness with life is not the same as detachment; soured disappointment with love or indifference to personal commitment is not the same as Christian chastity, and flowers and gardens do not rescue us from the desert of our material world nor do they help us to build that city which is the end product of the Christian view of evolution. Mindless spiritualism has about as much to do with Christian spirituality as the vow 'never to touch another drop' on the 'morning after the night before' has to do with true sobriety—it is simply a hangover! Indeed the obsession with spiritualism as a reaction against materialism is very dangerous indeed. It is one thing to be materialistic about material things, but to be materialistic about spiritual things is verging on the dangers of magic. It was precisely the sin of Simon Magus, and it is the continuing flaw in magic of every kind. To the pragmatic mind not concerned with truth but only with subjective pragmatism, there is always the temptation of Jesus in the wilderness to end up worshipping evil because it works and can produce the goods.

'Miraculous, prophetic phenomena, even if produced "in the name of Christ", are no guarantee of salvation,' writes Simon Tugwell. 'This is a hard saying for our success-minded generation, which almost automatically assumes that "if it works, it'll do." Unfortunately, however well it works, it may not do. The Antichrist as well as the Christians will work miracles, and, according to a legend of the Eastern Church (see Soloviev's *Tale of the Antichrist*), he will be a most successful churchman and leader of revival and reunion.' (*Did you receive the Spirit?* Simon Tugwell, OP)

For sadly it is not a long leap from this reaction against materialism into the bondage of blatant superstition. This is always the danger at such moments in history: a mindless, formless subjective religion, without structures, history or morals, indifferent to the tests of science, riddled with superstition and searching for some new experience or trip. The flood gates are wide open to everything from the demonic to the bizarre. 'When a man ceases to believe in God', says Chesterton, 'he does not believe in nothing: he believes in anything.' Superstition and sorcery—the new bondage of the new age, all bred from a weariness and disillusionment with an age of arid intellectual materialism.

> But what more oft in Nations grown corrupt;
> And by their vices brought to servitude,
> Than to love bondage more than liberty;
> Bondage with ease than strenuous liberty. (*Samson Agonistes*—Milton)

The other side of protest marches and political activism is so often the indifference of weariness in the name of idealism, and this rapidly feeds the flames of a new superstition, a new fundamentalism and a new bondage. The retreat of the popular secular mysticism from the arena of scientific truth and political combat is a retrograde step and has nothing to do with genuine Christian spirituality. It leads to that most dangerous of polarisations between Martha and Mary, between serpents and doves, between politics and ideals. It is a sickness which, at its best, Christianity has refuted in the name of a truly incarnational and sacramental spirituality. It is the sickness of a humpty-dumpty world of bits and pieces and schizoid behaviour in which creed and daily curriculum are totally disconnected.

Aldous Huxley, in his book *The Doors of Perception*, describes his transcendental experiences after taking the drug mescalin—the chemical short-cut to para-normal encounters. He writes significantly:

> But now I knew contemplation at its height. At its height, but not yet in its fullness. For in its fullness the way of Mary includes the way of Martha and raises it, so to speak, to its own higher power. Mescalin opens up the way of Mary, but shuts the door on

that of Martha. It gives access to contemplation—but to a contemplation that is incompatible with action and even with the will to action, the very thought of action.

Here is the polarisation which in every way traditional Christian spirituality with its central doctrine of the incarnation sternly resists. Sadly this is the very polarisation with which our contemporary world is faced: Martha versus Mary; the serpent versus the dove; the activist in political struggles versus the sitter-in or the marcher bathing in an untested idealism. For while the 'doves' squat or march, the 'serpents' walk up and down the corridors of power. Idealism which has no methodology will, as always before in history, soon be taken over by the unscrupulous and those who seek power for their own sakes. I would go further: the next step beyond superstition, the demonic and the bizarre is the promotion of hatred as a virtue in itself; the cult of the ugly and the profane. If this is so the prognosis for the eighties on both the social and political fronts is terrifying indeed.*

In Christian spirituality, theology, philosophy and politics there should be no room for such a polarisation. We need to distinguish here between things which look alike but which spring from different roots and end up at very different goals. For, at first sight Christianity and its spirituality could look very much like the protest of this secular mysticism. It is that old hardy of the difference between nearness by distance and nearness by approach. Secular mysticism and Christian spirituality may be very near by distance and look sometimes like peas out of the same pod, but by approach they are very different. This difference between nearness and likeness by distance and nearness and likeness by approach is a crucial part of Christian discernment most clearly portrayed in the writing of C. S. Lewis.

Perhaps an analogy may help. Let us suppose that we are doing

---

* It is in this context that I regard the writings of neo-Fascists in the paper of the National Front. 'The day our followers lose their ability to hate', wrote John Tyndall in *Spearhead* in September 1975, 'will be the day that they lose their power and their will to achieve anything worth while.'

a mountain walk to the village which is our home. At mid-day we come to the top of a cliff where we are, in space, very near it because it is just below us. We could drop a stone into it. But as we are no cragsmen we can't get down. We must go a long way round; five miles maybe. At many points during that detour we shall, statically, be far further from the village than we were when we sat above the cliff. But only statically. In terms of progress we shall be far 'nearer' our baths and teas. (*The Four Loves*)

The brash materialism of the fifties and the idealistic spiritualism of the seventies may look very far apart 'by distance' from each other, but in fact 'by approach' they are sadly very close. They are both pragmatic and man-centred. To be materialistic about material things is comparatively harmless, but to be materialistic about spiritual things is positively dangerous—it is at the very heart of Christ's own temptations in the wilderness. Unless between materialism and spiritualism there has been a real conversion, the last state can be worse than the first.

It is equally true that what looks by distance very close to Christian virtues can be a whole lifetime's journeying away from us by approach. Saintliness and immature naïvity might look very much alike but they are opposite poles of a long journey of growth and education. The power of the gospel is precisely its strange ability to separate what appears to be on the surface such obvious and comfortable bedfellows (see St Luke 17:34ff).

Yet the fact remains that few could have foreseen that the seventies would in fact be an era of many gods, many religions, esoteric and cultic. So in fact it is gnosticism which is the enemy of the Church today, not atheism or agnosticism. It is not the task of the Church today to contest belief in God (that was the apologetics of an earlier debate—a more arrogant, more adventuresome and in many ways a more healthy debate). Rather the task of the Church today is to proclaim and relate the particular and peculiar claims of a God who is incarnate in Christ—always a stumbling block to greeks, for there are always 'greeks' anxious for discussion in an age which is weary of action or commitment. The climate is not unlike that of Mars Hill again, and Paul did not find that the easiest of his platforms. The task is a difficult one, for while we should meet the secular mysticism as a new opportunity of a new passing phase, it will be important to redirect it if it is not ultimately to disintegrate and give way to even more demonic and terrifying manifestations of 'religion'.* Because of course, religion will not just disintegrate and disappear. It will change its form for some new fad, and history and commonsense might tell us some of the directions that unredeemed religion can take. For example in the face of indifference to structure, law and order and no real moral commitment, there will always be those who in the name of religion will wish to clean up and tidy up the nation and its morals. These are days when political extremes will flourish and win a ready audience. The long hair of the fifties and sixties could soon give way to short cut hair, training in gymnasia and the quest for the pure race. Paul Johnson in his *Enemies of Society* touches on this in a penetrating and convincing way.

Power religions thus encompass a variety of ideas, old and new, which have been forged into ferocious instruments of state tyranny. They ascribe to Nature, Biology, History or other abstractions many of the attributes which Christian theology ascribes to God. These abstractions are then presented as irresistible forces which the new state incarnates. Hence the Nazis deified the blood-force of the German race, which had an irresistible historical role to play for the next thousand years. They retained the old ruler-God worship of Hitler, and huge pseudo-religious public ceremonies. For the Nazi baptism service, a room was decorated with Nazi flags, the Tree of Life, branches of birch trees and candles and a centre altar contained a photograph of Hitler and a copy of *Mein Kampf....* Communist marriage ceremonies in Moscow's 'Palace of Weddings' are basically the same, though they vary in ostentation and price; Lenin gazes serenely on the couple from the walls, while an official administers oaths of loyalty to the Workers' State. Unlike Nazism, which rested on Nature-Biology, Communism claims its legitimacy from History, which replaces the salvation process, has God-like attributes

---

* I would see the use of neo-Fascism and Nazism as already evident in our society.

and is presented as essentially beneficent. The theology of the God-state is expanded or modified as required, to explain away new phenomena or incorporate new political objectives. (*Enemies of Society*)

Man is a compulsive worshipper and sooner or later his religious instincts will have their say. We ignore the power of religion at our peril as a civilisation. It will not go away; it will become converted or perverted. The penultimate enemy of man is religion and a society or civilisation which supposes that it has grown beyond religion and its needs is always the one most easily duped and most ready to revert to the horrors of primitive religious convictions and behaviour. Paul Johnson puts it at its most extreme when he summarises:

> The idea of religion disappearing is as illusory as that Marxist vision of the withering state. There will always be policemen, judges, gaolers—and clergymen of a kind. Better therefore priests, than witchdoctors. (*Enemies of Society*)

The opportunity and responsibility of catholic Christianity today

It was precisely the ability of catholic Christianity in past ages to meet the religious needs at such moments as these in history which created what we, with hindsight, like to call the ages of faith or the moments of religious revival. In the opening of the nineteenth century with its reaction against the age of rationalism and with the advent of romanticism (frequently accompanied also by drugs and chemically induced experiences) the revival of that period both started from where people were and then took them to where they would not otherwise have travelled. Perhaps the most striking parallel, however, is in the age of Augustine, in the crumbling years of the Empire leading up to the sack of Rome in A.D. 410, when the ancient world abounded with religions, superstition and sorcery, the weary indifference of *otium liberale*,* and yet when men like

---

* *Otium liberale* was seen by many of Augustine's contemporaries as the way of coping with such a world in disintegration. (See esp. Chapter 11 of *Augustine of Hippo.*)

Ambrose and Augustine, products of the age, saw in catholic Christianity a fuller and a richer way. In one sense the Church has been this way many times before. Paul Johnson summarises this with an abrasive confidence:

> The Roman republic and early empire was a market arena for a multitude of rival private religions, and it was the triumph of Christianity that it scooped the pool. The process could occur again, will in all probability recur ... and the sociologists have a good deal of evidence that we are now in a market phase. (*Enemies of Society*)

So it was that St Augustine of Hippo, shopping round the supermarket of religions, philosophies and politics of the Western world in the last quarter of the fourth century stumbled upon the genius of catholic Christianity.

> I no longer desired a better world, because I was thinking of creation as a whole: and in the light of this more balanced discernment, I had come to see that higher things are better than the lower, but that the sum of all creation is better than the higher things alone. (*Confessions, Bk VII*, xiii 19)

In a topsy-turvy world falling apart at the seams, the climate in which Augustine had carried out his explorations was one of disenchantment, disillusionment and retreat.†

Men, weary of the material world around them, had grown curious about another world of 'spiritual' things—the pursuit of an alternative culture over and against the hard claims of politics, power, wealth and moral decisions. In so many ways Augustine was the product of that age, torn in pieces by other competing claims upon his energies and concerns. In so many ways he was the idealist looking for 'a better world'—for 'higher things'—while at the same time he was immersed in, mesmerised by and enslaved to the con-

† For a full study of this climate of retreat which pervaded much of the world of the late antiquity, see the writings of Peter Brown, esp. *Augustine of Hippo* and *The World of Late Antiquity*.

tagious compensations of a crumbling empire and a fading culture. For Augustine, his discovery of catholic Christianity, as opposed to the dualism and gnosticism of much contemporary Manichaeanism, put together for the first time not only the pieces of the external world around him into a fuller and richer world-view, but it also brought together the pieces of his interior world and enabled him to put his life together with a single purpose and an overriding integrity. For catholic Christianity was not just about a better world of higher things. Philosophies and religions of that ilk will inevitably proliferate in such an age. For Augustine his pearl was a discovery of a far greater price. Here at last was a religion which claimed to be concerned not so much with the 'higher things' over and against the 'lower things', but something much better, much fuller and yet more elusive: 'the sum of all creation'. It claimed to bring glory under your feet.

It is dangerous to press historical parallels, yet in so far as mankind is consistent, history surely has some lessons to teach and some parallels to be drawn. What about the last quarter of the fourth century and that period leading up to the sack of Rome by the Goths in A.D. 410? For it was in that time scale and in that environment that Christianity emerged from a largely underground minority group into the most formative and influential force of its day. Strangely, however, it was not a case of Christianity versus blatant materialism: at its best Christianity does not draw such an over-simplified polarisation. It was a case rather of the distinctive marks and characteristics of catholic Christianity in a world which had become disillusioned by structures, responsibility and power, and was fleeing from these into the arms of superstitious, spiritual and gnostic religions which constituted the very atmosphere in which Christianity was to come into its own.

The claims of the new religions from the east were to by-pass the material world.* In a culture which had grown weary of thought forms; in a world of increasing lawlessness, inflation and licence

---

* The power of superstition and sorcery at this period is more fully dealt with in Peter Brown's collection of essays entitled: *Religion and Society in the Age of St Augustine* (see esp Part One, Sections four and five).

there were many who were all too ready to 'drop out' into the quieter life (*otium liberale* was the phrase used for this in the ancient world).

There were many who were only too willing to seek a way which would by-pass those very areas of frustration largely rooted in the visible, the tangible and the structured in the name of a religion of the Spirit, of superstition and the 'higher life'—that cleaner and purer environment which could not be invaded, touched, handled or tested (see 1 John 1) by the materialistic manipulation of mankind.

This is always the charm of gnosticism, and the principal enemy of catholic Christianity from New Testament times onwards has always been, not so much blatant agnosticism or atheism, but rather the clinical superiority of gnostic purity and detachment.

It was into such an environment that an Ambrose of Milan or an Augustine of Hippo found that for them Catholicism was far from being another 'spiritual option'; they were pitchforked by their faith in the unseen to become further involved in the world of the visible—although it seemed to be decaying around them. Such is the true test of the contemplative or indeed of all spiritual expeditions: it is the return journey which is the ultimate vindication of the reality and validity of the trip!†

In many ways then, catholic Christianity has been this way before, and makes its strongest appeal not so much against the hard pragmatic world of scientific humanism—though it should be ready for that debate also—but particularly in the realm of a supermarket of religious choices, and not least the soft options of gnosticism which always has such an immediate appeal at times like this in history. The challenge to the Church is clear. It must meet this persistent religious quest and redirect it to the fullness of the Gospel. 'Whatever may be said,' wrote Teilhard, 'our century is religious, probably more religious than any other; for how could it fail to be, with such a vast horizon before it and with such problems to be solved. The only problem is that our century has not the God it can adore.' Comment-

† Compare Gregory of Nazianzus on St Athanasius: 'He grew rich in contemplation, rich in splendour of life, combining them in wondrous sort by that golden bond that few can weave, using life as the guide of contemplation, contemplation as the seal of life.' (*Or. xxi*)

ing on this statement Suenens adds, 'We Christians who "see the glory of God shining in the face of Jesus" must bring this knowledge of the living God to those who search for Him' (*Future of the Church* page 102).

The challenge to catholic Christianity once again is to speak to an age in the bondage of religious taboos and fears, all too open to the dupes and delusions of bloodless gnosticism, and rapidly growing cold in love, about the fullness and warmth of that same richer quality of life which eventually won the heart and mind of an Ambrose of Milan or an Augustine of Hippo.

The power of catholic Christianity

To speak of catholic Christianity is of course to beg all the questions. It is not as though there were a body of thought clearly defined within a group of people standing in the wings waiting to be called into the drama of this 'religious age', holding a clear identity and ready to speak with a single voice. The churches are themselves in disarray, and perhaps at first we are tempted to look back to the early centuries and suppose that in the days of revival and missionary expansion the Church had done its homework on belief and Christian practice in preparation for the combat and the debate with the world of gnosticism and other religious sects. This is not so. All good theology is occasional theology, responding to a debate and an environment of decidedly opposing viewpoints. Orthodoxy, like good health, is not a thing you 'can have'. It is an ongoing contest and it is sometimes hard to tell which owes most to which. Theology is the cuckoo of the disciplines and lays all its best eggs in other people's nests. Catholic renewal will survive in an environment in which it will be compelled to dig deep and bring out of its treasure things new and old. Faith is not a thing we can have or lose; it is a daily response to our environment which must be renewed afresh each morning and which is developed in the light of each new day's experience.

Nevertheless this is not the same as saying that 'Christianity' is a word 'of so many meanings that it means nothing at all' (C. S. Lewis). It can embrace everything only because it first of all believes something. It never makes that mistake of setting out to be universal and ending up being élitist and exclusive. It is able to love everyone because it is first and foremost committed to loving Someone. It is so easy to fall in love with love and end up by loving no one except one's own projection of perfect love. The door to the universal is always particular and specific: the best preparation for the universal love of heaven is the purgatory of marriage on earth!

C. S. Lewis writes:

> Measured against the ages, 'mere Christianity'* turns out to be no insipid interdenominational transparency, but something positive, self-consistent and inexhaustible. I know it, indeed, to my cost. In the days when I still hated Christianity, I learned to recognise, like some all too familiar smell, that almost unvarying *something* which met me, now in Puritan Bunyan, now in Anglican Hooker, now in Thomist Dante. It was there (honeyed and floral) in Francois de Sales; it was there (grave and homely) in Spenser and Walton; it was there (grim but manful) in Pascal and Johnson; there again with a mild, frightening, Paradisial flavour, in Vaughan and Boehme and Traherne. In the urban society of the eighteenth century one was not safe—Law and Butler were two lions in the path. The supposed 'Paganism' of the Elizabethans could not keep it out; it lay in wait where a man might have supposed himself safest, in the very centre of The Faerie Queene and the Arcadia. It was of course varied; and yet—after all—so unmistakably the same; recognisable, not to be evaded, the odour which is death to us until we allow it to become life. (C. S. Lewis: *Introduction to St Athanasius on the Incarnation*)

Any renewal of catholic Christianity must be part of that 'tradition': it must feel to the touch to be of the same recognisable texture. One characteristic is certain: its total antipathy to all that is gnostic or merely sophisticated. There will be nothing 'sensible' or synthetic

---

* 'mere Christianity' is a phrase Lewis borrowed from Bishop Baxter who frequently uses it for mainstream Christianity—what most Christians have believed most of the time.

about catholicism. Of course an age like our own—or that of
Augustine—deeply aware that it has soiled the substance of creation
and polluted the environment of all its exchanges, would like to
splinter off, and start again. That is the immediate appeal of gnosticism in its many forms: a fresh start six feet above the sordid earth.
But in catholic Christianity the diagnosis and the cure, the problem
and the solution are firmly rooted in the earth of the created order
and it offers no solution which seeks to by-pass the created order.
Rather, redemption is firmly anchored in that most touchy area
where the problem is most acute: flesh and blood, matter and materialism, sexuality and personality; the bread of daily diet and the
wine of drunken festivity. All these are the roots of that Tree of Life,
firmly planted in the earth of history in order that it may fully
blossom in the heaven of eternity: glory, but always under your feet.
There is continuity as well as discontinuity between Creation and
Redemption; between the pull of nature and the freedom of grace.
Both alike are rooted in one and the same Person: the Second Person
of the Trinity. St Athanasius reminds us:

> The renewal of creation has been wrought by the Self-same Word
> Who made it in the beginning. There is no inconsistency between
> creation and salvation; for the One Father has employed the same
> Agent for both works, effecting the salvation of the world
> through the same Word Who made it at the first. (*De Incarnatione
> verbi Dei*)

Fifteen hundred years later another writer puts the same truth in
different language:

> Love cannot and must not dispense with matter, any more than
> can the soul. Just as Spirit is never so enfranchised from matter as
> to be able to reject it, so every union of love must begin on the
> material basis of sensible confrontation and knowledge. It is a
> fundamental law of creative union that the fusion of spiritual
> apexes presupposes a coincidence of their bases. (*The Eternal
> Feminine* by Henri de Lubac)

The challenge of catholic christology is that it is rooted in the incarnation: the challenge of catholic spirituality is that it is rooted in the sacramental. Both alike in seeking the fusion of 'spiritual apexes' are not ashamed to begin with the 'coincidence of their bases'. Such is the power of catholic Christianity to speak to that very area where the problem begins—that is the point of joining and of identification, and yet of course it is the most painful and difficult place to begin. It is a threat to the gnostic: it is all too ugly for the aesthete: it is too open to the risk of pollution for the idealist.

Any catholic renewal in the life of the Church will be brought about by this kind of abrasive involvement with the current tide of religious reaction. It must meet that tide but not simply float along with it.

> The renewal of catholicsm in the Church of England, as in the rest of the Christian world, is the recovery of wholeness. Catholic means whole. integral, complete: its opposite is partial, unbalanced, sectarian. Today, as we see the decay of narrow and inadequate forms of Christianity, and the revival of pietistic and harmful byways of belief, the renewal of catholic truth and life will not occur without a struggle. But it is essential if the true God is to be preached. (from the *Manifesto for Catholic Renewal* 1977)

The pages of this book are an attempt to outline the areas in which that struggle will take place. It is a vast over-simplication, but is still worth using as a model to speak of three main areas throughout the centuries which have been the focus of Christian controversy: all alike are to do with the nature of the Body of Christ. There are the christological controversies of the first five hundred years of Christianity. There are the eucharistic controversies of the Middle Ages and the Reformation: and today there are the controversies around the nature of the Church, the sacrament of baptism and the question: 'What is a Christian?' In many ways these are three aspects of one and the same basic mystery: Corpus Christi. The way we answer one of these issues will affect the way we answer the other two. The way we experience one of these three aspects should invade our theology of the other two. The nature of the Church is the central theme of so much of today's theological controversies. It manifests itself through the discussions around the nature of Christian initiation, the question of authority and the nature of Christian living and morality. All three aspects of this one central mystery involve struggle and faith, but perhaps it is in the third aspect—the nature of the Church—that the mystery comes uncomfortably close with a reality which is hard to bear. 'We are the Body of Christ.'

In the course of the pages of this book we shall look at the main characteristics of the Church as listed in the creeds: one, holy, catholic and apostolic. They will serve as useful guidelines to a wide-ranging discussion. The purpose of that discussion is not merely academic. It is intended to point readers to the ingredients of renewal which alone can equip catholic Christianity today for the challenge of the contemporary crisis—a religious crisis, which is not simply the property of ecclesiastical squabbles, but rather a crossroad for the survival of civilisation.

2. RENEWAL IN HOLINESS

Christianity and goodness

The test of catholic Christianity is not so much whether or not it can make good men better, but whether or not it can make bad men holy. The Church rightly proclaims as an act of faith that it is a holy Church, yet to the 'man in the street' there is a crisis of credibility about this statement, 'I'm as good as those who go to church.' He sees the Church in purely functional terms as being there basically to help people to be better. The very word 'Christian' has become synonymous with the word 'good'. It is hardly surprising, therefore, that since people who go to church are evidently neither much better nor much worse than those who do not, the Church is dismissed as useful for those who happen to like that kind of thing but as failing enormously in producing the goods for which it is supposedly in business. Although this is largely a superficial assessment it frequently goes much further because it has to be admitted that many people who do not 'come to church' stay away because they know they break the commandments and they expect that the Church is primarily for good people who keep the commandments. Such people—and they are often idealists with high principles—are in turn deeply shocked when they meet a Christian (and even more a priest) who clearly does not live up to Christian ideals and they are then compelled to speak of hypocrisy and of not 'practising what we preach'.

I really believe that this matter is no small issue because in the end it has far-reaching implications both for those who are active members of the Church and for those who are not. Holiness, rightly understood, is at the heart of renewal in the Church today. Its meaning and its implications are enormous. The Church will continue to be in the Western world an unrepresentative ghetto unless and until it can reassert its own identity as being rooted in holiness rather than goodness—an identity which is more evident in weakness rather than in strength and more eloquent in failure rather than in success (see 1 Corinthians 1:25–29).

It is this emphasis which broke through the armour of St Paul who had been rendered brittle by the Law, seeking to achieve a self-righteousness and a self-justifying identity. For him it was the realisation of God's strength in his weakness and Christ's victory in his defeat that brought him to experience wholeness and holiness. It must be a similar emphasis which alone can break through the sham protection of liberal moral failure which haunts our Western world in the name of love and kindness. For strangely enough it is the permissive secular world which faces a moral crisis. It has sought to rid itself of the dogma of the Church but the tyrant of popular opinion has proved to be far more censorious in moral matters than ever the Church has been throughout its history. A liberal attitude in morals has a strange knack of richocheting! We can all too easily find that we have exchanged the frying pan of objective Christian morality for the fire of public opinion on matters of 'acceptable' moral behaviour. It was never the Church, when it held power either in the Middle Ages or in Victorian England, that dismissed men from public office for adultery, fornication or even minor misdemeanours of the wrong handling of public money. It is a strange 'liberal' climate that demands that its public leaders must permit their private lives to be scrutinised by the press and other media in the name of honesty and that they should then be dismissed unless they are found to be perfect and without blemish in those areas in which the popular conscience is most sensitive at any particular time. There is a new and selective moral indignation abroad which, like a virus, can wipe out a whole civilisation if it is not checked; and yet to check it would require a swing to one of two extremes: either on the one hand into utter moral chaos or on the other a reaction into puritanical moralism.

An inverted moralism

For the truth is that the moral climate of the post-Christian world is an unhealthy one. It is not a world with no morality but rather, like a prison, it is a world with a highly selective morality. When a man ceases to believe in God and in his moral laws he does not cease to have a moral code but instead he creates his own moral code with a censorious self-hatred and judgementalism which far exceeds even the sternest of Christian apologists for the moral life. This process of moral decadence is ugly and hideous for at the heart of it is a deep self-hatred on the one hand, and a self-righteous justification on the other.

For it is not only true for Christians that they have sinned and fallen short of the glory of God: even the atheist or agnostic (and worse still the post-Christian) is very conscious of falling short of his own moral standards or inherited goals of behaviour. The difference for the Christian is that the one who sets the standards, also forgives and loves us in our weakness and failure: 'as is his judgement, so is his mercy'. That alone can lead to a true self-loving based on the experience of grace which transcends even the awareness of our weaknesses. This is the basis of St Paul's personal breakthrough, releasing enormous energies in a new understanding of a true self-love and proper self-regard which are in turn at the root of all real freedom.

The Christian religion can begin for a man or a woman only when a proper self-love and self-regard have been learned. We are told in the Scriptures to love our neighbour *as* ourselves and not more than ourselves. But then if we do not love God first because he loves us, we shall necessarily distort and pervert our loving into a self-justifying ordinance in which we isolate various moral attitudes giving them a tyrannical power far greater than anything that ever came out of Sinai. Mrs Fidget in C. S. Lewis's *Four Loves* is the contemporary figure in family life, politics and the protest movements of our age. She had high ideals and she claimed to put her family long before herself and to live for them.

I am thinking of Mrs Fidget, who died a few months ago. It is really astonishing how her family have brightened up. The drawn look has gone from her husband's face; he begins to be able to laugh. The younger boy, whom I had always thought an embittered peevish little creature, turns out to be quite human. The elder, who was hardly ever at home except when he was in bed, is nearly always there now and has begun to reorganise the garden. The girl, who was always supposed to be 'delicate' (though I never found out what exactly the trouble was), now has the riding lessons which were once out of the question, dances all night, and plays any amount of tennis. Even the dog who was never allowed out except on a lead is now a well-known member of the Lamp-post Club in their road. Mrs Fidget very often said that she lived for her family and it was not untrue. Everyone in the neighbourhood knew it. 'She lives for her family,' they said, 'what a wife and mother!' She did all the washing; true, she did it badly, and they could have afforded to send it out to a laundry, and they frequently begged her not to do it. But she did. There was always a hot lunch for anyone who was at home and always a hot meal at night (even in midsummer). They implored her not to provide this. They protested almost with tears in their eyes (and with truth) that they liked cold meals. It made no difference. She was living for her family. She always sat up to 'welcome' you home if you were out late at night; two or three in the morning, it made no odds; you would always find the frail, pale, weary face awaiting you, like a silent accusation. . . . For Mrs Fidget, as she so often said, would 'work her fingers to the bone' for her family. They couldn't stop her. Nor could they—being decent people—quite sit still and watch her do it. They had to help. That is, they did things for her to help her to do things for them which they didn't want done. . . . The Vicar says Mrs Fidget is now at rest. Let us hope she is. What's quite certain is that her family are.

Any virtue in isolation from a proper self-love and self-regard is precisely the destructive element which Lewis so humorously and yet so tellingly describes.

It is very dangerous indeed to 'live for others'. An age which has dispensed with the love of God will end by making our neighbour or a cause a new god demanding our love and service while harbouring a deep self-hatred. The mark of service is joy and only those who first know that they are loved are free to serve others in the joyful expression of that interior knowledge of first being loved. 'Herein is love, not that we love God, but that he first loved us.' Without that interior knowledge we are not free to love others or to serve them, for we must first love ourselves. Without this prime realisation of a true self-love we shall end up by hating both ourselves and others.

For unredeemed man is always moralistic but in that most dangerous and selective way. In a prison there are criminals who are heroes for the crimes that they have committed, and there are criminals who are despised for the crimes that they have committed. The prison house is not an amoral community it is a highly censorious community with a deep sense of what is 'right' and what is 'wrong'. In a similar way each age has its selective morality. The nineteenth century was prudish, for example, about sexual morality while being permissive and indulgent about property and privilege. The twentieth century is prudish about property and privilege and permissive and indulgent about sexual morality. The parallels are fascinating. We would claim with hindsight that while many people lived lives of chastity both in and out of marriage during the nineteenth century there was much hypocrisy about sexual behaviour and a tendency to regard all sexual behaviour as 'dirty'. The worst sin for the Victorians seemed to be those sins associated with sexual behaviour—the sin of lust—while we are of course aware (with a dangerous superiority) of other Victorian failings which would seem to us much more devastating and destructive. But perhaps the twenty-first century will look back (with equal superiority) and see our society regarding property and privilege as though they were in themselves something 'dirty' with all the hypocrisy and double thinking which plagued the Victorians in their attitude to sexual morality. They may well say of us that while we placed at the top of our social ills the misuse and indulgence of property and privilege we were blind to other sins and weaknesses all too evident to those who have the privilege of hindsight. Some are called to celibacy as a voluntary way of fulfilment and all are called to chastity. Some are called to poverty as a voluntary way of fulfilment but all are called to a right ordering of their possessions and privileges. But in both matters of sexuality and property and riches, judgementalism is wrong. It is a dangerous game to play the keeper of one's brother's conscience. 'Judge not, that ye be not judged' is a self-evident and sensible command to any society unless it is to tear itself apart through moralism and judgementalism.

Self-justification

Perhaps the worst feature of post-Christian moralism is its self-justifying nature. It is hideous to see a person who has never grown up to be a 'good loser'. Little children always want to 'win', and sometimes half-way through the game they will knock the chess-board over rather than lose, or worse still rewrite the rules in order to make sure of winning. Of course it is understandable in a child (and even more in a spoilt child): it is hideous in a grown-up or in society at large. The lovely thing about being a Christian is that you do not have to win. Furthermore you do not have to write the rules or even agree with them all but rather realise that without the rules there is no game and the referee does not always have to be right! The Christian does not have to be right and he does not have to win: but he does have to be forgiven.

Situational ethics is a genuine attempt to relate circumstances to rules, but it is so often in danger of toppling over into a subtle form of self-justification. To be convinced of sin is not the worst thing that can happen to a man, but to miss the opportunity of the experience of forgiveness, or to attempt to rewrite the rules in the name of a spirit of generous realism, may well miss the point of it all and leave the Church with a new and more dangerous form of moralism. Of course moral theology must always be under review in a process which involves a tension between the Bible, tradition and reason informed by a Holy Spirit which is at work as well in the world as in the Church. But in the end, moral theology belongs together with ascetical theology in which both compassion on the one hand and an even more demanding set of rules on the other can apply in any one situation. The Church is not an institution primarily concerned with morals but rather with discipleship and enabling men and women to draw closer to God in Christ. Such a process inevitably involves judgement but in the New Testament judgement and mercy go hand in hand. At some point on that journey (ascetical theology), compassion and understanding will be most in evidence (the woman taken in adultery). At other points there will be stern demands which, unless they are met, render further growth and development impossible (eg the rich young ruler). In the New Testament moral theology and ascetical theology go hand in hand and converge at that point of living encounter with Christ. But that point is always a moment of repentance, forgiveness and renewal and is a million light-years away from self-justification and the desire to win or to be right after all.

Self-justification is an ugly feature in a moralistic society, which cannot cope with failure because it has never experienced forgiveness. Forgiveness is at the heart of holiness as holiness in its turn is a distinctive feature of Christianity. A Church which is not holy will not be catholic and a Church which is catholic can only be so because it has found the secret of holiness. The Church must be representative of the good and the bad and the indifferent and as many sided as society itself, yet it will never achieve that spectrum of membership if it is selective in moralistic terms and invites men and women to bring only their strengths and their goodness to God. It is rather their weakness and their failures which draw men and women to forgiveness and make possible the gift of holiness. We are not asked to believe in a good Church: we must profess belief in a holy Church. In a climate of self-justifying moralism—and that is never very far from a permissive society—the Church needs again to discover the power and experience of holiness through forgiveness. In a climate seduced by, or over-reacting against, materialism, the Church needs to proclaim afresh a whole view of man and the universe in the process of Redemption through Incarnation. One holy, catholic and apostolic Church is no mere credal formula of an institution: it is the flesh and blood reality which carries with it good news, fulfilment and a richer life.

Unless we discover the secret of Redemption through forgiveness, we shall be compelled to reject much of the world and much of ourselves. The world and ourselves will become like the curate's egg—'good in parts'!

Teilhard de Chardin in his book *Le Milieu Divin* demonstrates how unredeemed man is trapped within three options in his response to the world around him—he will be distorted, disgusted or divided. The material world, the vastness of the universe around him, or the unchartered depths of the world within him, delude man and disappoint him, giving rise to all kinds of religious and philosophical attitudes falling into one of these three categories; distortion, disgust, or division.

All too easily we are distorted by the world and its claim upon us. We would all like to be universalists, and in that sense catholicism in so far as it means universal has a natural appeal. However, in catholicism we arrive at the universal through the narrow door of particularity. The sad reality is that those who set out to love the world and to accept it in its totality end up by being the most parochial and the most selective. Most of this distortion is the inevitable result of being caught up by one part of life—mistaking the part for the whole. In a vast universe without religions or philosophical maps, where myths are despised and symbolism has been intellectualised, there is no way of relating the part to the whole, and specialisation inevitably leads to alienation. 'They walk one road to set them free, and find they've gone the wrong direction' (Don Maclean *Crossroads*). It is not only that society around us is fragmented into a competitive jungle, but also that the world within us registers conflicting evidence as head and heart, intellect and intuition oscillate between playing the role first of tyrant and then of serf. There is no perspective or proportions, only distorted figures chasing first one fad and then another.

Little wonder that under such conditions many are just repelled and disgusted by the world and its claims upon them and that many reject the material world in that flight for the 'spiritual'. Scratch a materialist, and not far below the surface you will find the gnostic and the aesthete vying for pride of place. The contemporary fad of rejecting structures and institutions, materialistic involvement and the sciences is a recurring theme, and many will band-wagon religion in their disgust with the results of former habits of over-indulgence and materialistic obsession. Manichaeanism is never far from us if we are on the brink of materialism, and much that parades as Christian spirituality is in fact Manichaeanism in disguise.

The religion of the Incarnation if preached and practised is abhorrent to the self-styled spiritual idealist, but sadly the Church is frequently duped by such people who turn the catholic religion of Christ to their own advantage, spiritualising away the history of Jesus in flesh-and-blood terms in the name of theological sophistication. It is no accident that in the gnostic climate of the first century the acid test of catholic Christianity was to confess that Jesus had come in the flesh (see 1 John 4:2, 3). In this rejection of the world, as it is, in the name of the world, as it should be, there is no continuity between Creation and Redemption but rather the superimposing of a self-justifying moralism upon a volcano of passions which are unresolved and unattended.

For most mortals, however, the way is less dramatic and less single minded, and is neither wholly disgust nor wholly distortion but rather sheer division. Most people in fact are divided, 'halting between two opinions' (see 1 Kings 18:21), fearing to test either and torn in two by both. 'You cannot serve God and Mammon'—no, you can't because in the end you will end up by hating both. The schizoid is the classic pattern with Hyde and Jekyll unrelated and unreconciled, each making his alternate appearance and in the end destroyed by their division. 'A house divided against itself cannot stand.' How often in pastoral encounters the priest finds himself caught in that impossible division with a person who insists for example on being spiritual about his eroticism and erotic about his spirituality! Such a person can never be recollected in a single presence because they always plead the cause from the point of view of 'the other side of the fence'. This is of course the most comfortable way to plead any cause because it is where the grass is always greener and where the adage 'if only' is the eternal excuse for never 'getting it together'. Little wonder that James in his epistle reminds us that a 'double-minded man' cannot receive anything from God: of course he cannot because he is never 'quite all there' to receive it. However accommodating God may be in his wish to give to man his many and good gifts, man must first desire with his *whole* heart and with all his passions before he can fully be fed and fully receive. Stability is therefore highly placed in the vows of St Benedict, for only so can many people in the end be 'cornered' in a way which makes possible both collision and conversion.

The permutations of Teilhard's three 'Ds' are many, but they lead to indecision and in the end to paralysis. The appetite becomes jaded and fades, and such a generation, far from going too far, never goes far enough. That is the definition of sin—not that we went too far, but rather that we never went far enough: we never hit the target but rather fall short in the 'decadence' of fatigue and loss of direction, never going out 'with a bang' but rather 'with a whimper' (T. S. Eliot).

So decadence is literally the word which describes our contemporary moral climate. This is not the generation of explorers and those who kick over the traces. It is the generation of the decadent, for decadence by definition is that which falls short and returns in ever-decreasing circles back upon itself. The maps may get bigger, but the vision gets smaller, as patriotism refuses to give way to internationalism and reverts to something little better than parochial tribalism. It is all too easy to describe the present climate as permissive because that might suggest the freedom to explore and to break loose. It is much more accurate to describe it as decadent even if the word has painful associations. Decadence is not that lust for life summarised in the eternal protest of Oliver Twist—'please Sir I want some more!' Decadence is a weariness with life which leaves most of the meal on the plate through boredom or indifference. The sin of twentieth-century man will never be that he loved himself too much but rather that he did not love himself enough.

> It would seem that Our Lord finds our desires not too strong but too weak. We are half-hearted creatures, fooling about with drink and sex and ambition when infinite joy is offered us, like an ignorant child who wants to go on making mud pies in a slum because he cannot imagine what is meant by the offer of a holiday at the sea. We are far too easily pleased. (C. S. Lewis *The Weight of Glory*)

A yet more excellent way
The Church's teaching on Redemption to holiness through forgive-

ness is a fuller option than any that the world could ever offer. It weaves its way between moralism on the one hand and permissiveness on the other; between indifference and judgementalism; in a fuller option than any of the ways of distortion, division or disgust. It is a way which is moral without being moralistic, and because it accepts the judgement of God first it need have no truck with the judgementalism of men. Such a way has no need of self-justification because the one who judges also justifies and the one who knows all is ready to forgive all. It is a 'yet more excellent way' 'towering o'er the wrecks of time'; and a renewal of the Church in its understanding of its own calling to holiness would in its turn also bring a new evangelistic and pastoral concern for the world. The challenge first to the Church itself to recover again both its understanding and experience of holiness as being a 'yet more excellent way' than any of the other choices open to mankind, must have pride of place in the agenda for the Church in our present age.

For holiness and goodness as we have seen are not the same and often the latter is not the best breeding ground for the former. The good man who is by nature good and loving is frequently good in his own strength and far less open to the grace and strength of God than the weak man who knows his need of strength beyond his own resources. In fact it may not be going too far to say the Englishman's disease is goodness and, as surely as the enemy of the best is the good rather than the bad, so in many ways natural goodness is far more the enemy of holiness than blatant evil. All men are endowed with natural goodness to a greater or lesser extent. Natural virtue is part of the givenness of our life and rather like our parents, our IQ, the colour of our eyes or our hair; it is something of which we should neither be proud nor ashamed. It is very largely true that we love with the love with which we have been loved and if life stops there then the world is no better off for it is not until we are able to put back in more than we have taken out from a resource of love beyond what is natural that we begin to be 'profitable servants'. It is the unique reversal of catholic Christianity whereby the first and the last in this process are strangely interchangeable. There is more joy over one man who knows he is a sinner and is in need of that divine resource of renewal through forgiveness than over ninety and nine just persons who feel they have no need of repentance, forgiveness or renewal.

Little wonder that Paul reflecting on the constituency of the congregation of Corinth could comment that not many of them were strong according to this world's categories. Little wonder that the man in the street who may be quite a good chap will compare those who go to church and those who don't unfavourably by saying that he's as good as those who go to church. He may well be much better but he is in a different ball game, where the rules are different and where there are different starting points and quite different goals. Our society could be stuffed with 'good eggs' but the trouble with good eggs is that if they don't hatch they go bad!

Break-down, break-through and break-out are related processes for it is often those who are most broken down to whom God's grace and strength can best break through.

> How else except through broken heart
> May Lord Christ enter in? (Oscar Wilde *Ballad of Reading Gaol*)

The strength of God breaks through our self-sufficiency best in the weakness of our moments of break-down, for God's strength is made perfect in man's weakness and God's strength is at its most glorious and perfect in the wholeness and holiness of weak and frail humanity. Jesus was glorified at his weakest and most vulnerable moment—on the Cross, with heart broken and with blood and water pouring forth in that rush of love which alone makes possible the apostolic break-out in mission and true evangelism. 'The glory of God is man come alive' (Irenaeus).

For the mystery of holiness goes further—it goes right to the heart of man's origin and his destiny. According to the teaching of the Bible, the doctrine of the Church and experience of man—and these three evidences singularly agree on this point—forgiveness (and holiness) is more wonderful than innocency. Man restored by grace to the likeness of God is more wonderful than man made in the image of God in his first innocency.

> Nay had the apple taken been,
> The apple taken been.

Our Lady ne'er been heavenly queen.
Blessed be the time
That apple taken was! (Medieval carol)

This is dangerous stuff indeed, yet the Middle Ages frequently spoke of *felix culpa* and in the liturgy of Holy Saturday in the Exultet, the Church is not ashamed to sing about that 'happy sin'. 'O happy fault, O necessary sin of Adam, which gained for us so great a Redeemer.' Paul is so insistent to emphasise precisely this aspect of our Redemption, that he has to check himself: 'Shall we sin more then that grace may abound; no, God forbid' (Romans 6:1). In the Epistle to the Hebrews man restored is above the angels, while man in his original innocence was a little lower than the angels. Here is a new hierarchy which turns self-made man upside down so that the same door which sin closed against God is precisely the very door through which repentance makes possible the re-entry of God's grace to the very heart of our lives. Put another way, making it up after a row evokes even more love and demands that we go deeper beneath the superficial scar which has caused the initial break-down in our relationship. With foresight, innocency is better than sin, and in that sense we must strive to do the good and reject the bad. However—and here is the mystery—with hindsight forgiveness and sanctity are better than goodness in its own strength, and it is that very forgiveness which opens the door to new and deeper experiences of love and of God.

For Jesus himself reminds us that those who are forgiven much will love much and those who are forgiven little will love little. The failure of the Church is not its failure to be good but rather its failure to teach and experience forgiveness and the measure of the love of the Church will be precisely the measure of its own experience of forgiveness and holiness.

A holy Church is essential in any renewal of the Church, and at the heart of that holiness is obedience and necessarily forgiveness through repentance. For the opposite to this is a jaundiced Pelagianism, a self-justifying goodness which is as unattractive as it is unloving. Dare we go further? Could it be that because the Church has forgotten the quest of holiness and settled for 'good eggs' that it has lost its true character as the Body of Christ. It is only when we can uncover the features of the authentic Body of Christ beneath the debris and rubble of a self-made religion and a self-styled morality that Christ himself will be raised again for our world and lifted up in order to 'draw' all men to himself.

It is not insignificant that in the popular musical *Godspell* in the story of the Prodigal Son there is one serious textual inaccuracy. In the account of this story in St Luke, the Prodigal Son rehearses his speech as he decides to return to his father. It consists of three points: the acknowledgement of sin ('Father, I have sinned against heaven and before thee'); the realisation of unworthiness ('and am not worthy to be called thy son'); the wish to change his status in order to make a new start ('make me as one of thy hired servants'). When the father receives him into his arms, the son repeats the first two clauses but (and this is contrary to the text of *Godspell*) he does not repeat the third statement. The father on the contrary brings out a ring for his finger and shoes for his feet to endorse the unchangeable status of his sonship. This young man must realise that he is a son—a bad son, yes—but a son and now a forgiven son. The boy would like to have changed his status; he would have preferred to be an unforgiven slave who was quite good rather than a forgiven son who was really not much good. The enemy of this process was naturally the other son—the good one, the 'good egg'.

There in a nutshell is the scene so often re-enacted except, sadly, it is the churches which are so often peopled with outraged good people when they should really be full of forgiven bad people. Self-justifying will always opt to 'exchange his glory' (change its status) and redefine the rules so that we can more or less accept ourselves as quite good 'slaves'. The man in the street would rather be a good chap who doesn't go to church than a bad man who accepts his sonship and lives within the generosity of forgiveness. The younger brother had to learn that most painful lesson that it is no use trying to change our status but rather that we should realise and accept that we are sons, however bad, and yet sons who have experienced forgiveness. It is this which sometimes compels me to go as far as saying that we need more 'bad' Christians—Christians who know they are forgiven sons and daughters of God—rather than self-justifying good people who feel they have no need of repentance. If only Christian congregations looked a little more like a tableau of the cross-section of Chaucer's Canterbury Pilgrims (the good, the bad, the indifferent and the holy) and a little less like a crowd of people of whom it could only be said that in the end they never did anyone any harm. The nettle we have to grasp is that 'now are we the sons of God and it does not yet appear what we shall be'. In that sense we are hypocrites! We are claiming to be what we have not yet attained, and yet it is only by holding on to that ultimate status that we shall ever become what God intends us to be. The greatest enemy to this process is the process of self-justification, and self-made men.

The acceptance of our sonship—albeit unworthy, unearned and not self-evident—is the beginning of true renewal. But at the heart of that experience must be true repentance. Sanctity is God glorified in men. It is not just repair or renovation. It is the wonderful blend of continuity and discontinuity; it is Creation come alive in Redemption; it is the wholesome union of grace with nature without division, disgust or distortion, without confusion or absorption; it is a new Creation; it is 'the Lord's doing and it is marvellous in our eyes.'

'Problems are solutions in disguise: Magellan discovered the world was round by sailing closer to the edge than anyone else before him.' These words on an Underground poster have haunted me over many years. Repentance does not remove the problem but turns the problem to a point of new opportunity whereby it is also the secret of its own solution. The scar of sin is not removed: it becomes a glorious scar incorporated into the new design which includes and transcends the old pattern. Redemption is not a second plan annihilating the former plan of Creation: it is the first plan more gloriously executed, not in spite of the obstacles but through them and because of them. There is no going back to the garden of our innocency: we can only go on to the city of our sanctity in which the scars of our sins have become the main features of the pervading architecture through repentance and renewal. We are not to be second-class angels we are to be first-class saints.

In such edifices the old is not rejected but even our fantasies are realised in ways we had never suspected. There is no complete break between the old Creation and the new; the raw material of the old Adam and the characteristics of the new. It is the same drive of love redirected. Augustine summarises it so:

> Love cannot be idle. What is it that moves absolutely any man even to do evil, if it is not love? Show me a love that is idle and doing nothing. Scandals, adulteries, crimes, murders, every kind of excess, are they not the work of love? Cleanse your love, then. Divert into the garden the water that was running down the drain... (Augustine *Enarr. 11* in Psalm 31:5).

Our weaknesses have become our strengths and our defeats the very raw material of our true success. What we gave up for a while we have been able to keep for ever together with so very much more, and even our very needs have become God's opportunities to draw us even closer to himself. The saints on earth have been signs of this most remarkable process and we have rightly called them holy men and holy women. In their own hearts they have been most conscious of sin and failure, but even more conscious of the love and forgiveness of God and of his victory through weakness. They were frequently little men, often tempted to try to become big men, but through God's grace in the end they were truly great men.

Pastoral reflections and applications for today

> Faith is the affirmation and the act
> which binds eternal truth to present fact. (Coleridge)

The identity of the Church is to be the environment and community of faith which enables broken and divided humanity to hold together eternal truth and present realities. The man in the street would urge us to be only realistic, sensible, and existentialist, claiming to be neither more nor less than our unaided efforts could achieve. He would urge us to rewrite our ultimate and eternal destiny around our own moral achievements and so avoid that hypocrisy of which he is so often compelled to speak when he sees church-goers behaving in ways which are contrary to the Christian profession. Strangely enough the man in the street is joined here by much modern liberal theology—even situational ethics—which would want moral theology to be tailored to what is realistic in present circumstances. The weight of this argument, whether it is propounded by the secular pragmatist or the contemporary Christian reductionist, is its immediacy and seeming honesty; he could never be regarded as pretentious but rather would claim to face the world as it is in a spirit of honest pragmatism. Here indeed is down-to-earth religion!

The opposite end of the spectrum is another pair of equally unlikely bed-fellows—so heavenly minded as to be of no earthly use! There is a dangerous brand of Calvinistic Protestantism which would see conversion as a once-for-all turning away from sin and sins—a clean break with the past, with all that binds the new Creation to the old, the work of grace annihilating the natural man and creating a new Adam six feet above the earth with the feet of an angel, unclogged with mud and unpolluted with the former habits of a lifetime. Such a view of Christian perfectionism leaves no room for what St Augustine referred to so tellingly (and so painfully) as *consuetudino carnalis*—the familiar habits of the flesh and of a life lived purely in terms of the flesh. For such people chastity while not being necessarily confused with virginity is nevertheless regarded as being the same as sexual continence and leaves no room (or precious little) for post-conversion lapses. Strangely linked with this group would be the new secular mystic despising the earth one moment yet relying upon its props the next; pretending that man can achieve an identity which transcends the clay of worldly reality and fleeing from the city and the market place back to the garden, flowers and a purer environment. Both the Calvinist and the contemporary secular mystic tend to emphasise only discontinuity with man's roots, for both alike have rejected the paradox and contradictions which alone make possible an ultimate synthesis of the old with the new, of earth with heaven, and of what is now and what is yet to be. In a word, that synthesis is wholeness and holiness and it is the stuff of which saints are made.

The way of holiness in catholic Christianity is to hold together by faith this paradox in an often repeated act of faith. '*Now* are we the sons of God and it does not yet appear what we shall be' (1 John 3:2). The 'now' and the 'not yet' are bound in a single whole and held together by that reaffirmation of what was once-for-all proclaimed by God in Christ historically, and personally and individually appropriated at our baptism. For baptism is that once-for-all statement of God's love for me and his total acceptance of me in Christ. That alone is the point of departure for all explorations and wrong turnings. That is the point of return when we are lost and can no longer reaffirm ourselves or even know who we are.

The sacramental life is an extension of that once-for-all overriding reality. Whether I become on earth the most saintly Christian or whether I am a scoundrel and a bad Christian, I can never be more than the once-for-all statement that baptism made me and I can never undo what it once did for me. The sacraments were made for man and not man for the sacraments. God does not need them: we do. And so the Church is that community and environment in which the once-for-all may be often renewed. My sins cannot detract from it, and my virtues cannot add to it. It is true that in Christ (through baptism) a man is a new creation. But Creation (whether the first or the new creation) is not a single bang but an unfolding process in which God and men, grace and nature co-operate in an unfolding mystery for which there is no better word in our vocabulary than glory—the weight of glory.

Holiness is the evidence of that process. 'Holiness is always easier now,' writes Newman. That is the only urgency about this process, namely that it is less painful to say 'yes' to God *now* than it will be if I delay until tomorrow. At every point whenever I say 'yes' and reaffirm the baptismal statement, the mystery of my true self in Christ is uncovered and rediscovered. It is a mystery precisely because I cannot define it for myself—it is truly hid in the mind and heart of God. 'Hid with Christ in God' (Col 3:3). Whenever I say 'no' it is hell-on-earth; whenever I question it or 'halt' between two opinions, it is purgatory; whenever I am able by God's grace to surrender and share in Christ's 'yes' without any qualification, it is heaven-on-earth, and the Lord's own prayer is re-enacted in and through me for that moment.

For most of us, most of the time, the post-baptismal life is purgatory. Some people, some of the time, in some areas of their lives are able to say 'yes' to God in word and deed and will. Most of us, most of the time, in most areas of our life are only able to say 'maybe' to God in word and deed. We can only affirm him through our will and we need the opportunities to express that will and to re-establish the course and direction of our lives. Peter, once upon a time, three times said, 'No, I do not know him.' He said this both in action and in word. And so the great love of Christ contrives that precious occasion in St John's Gospel in the twenty-first chapter, when Peter, who had three times denied, could three times confess and re-orientate his will—'Lord, you know all things, you know that I love you.' It is true that that occasion is to some extent contrived and it is equally true that many times Peter between Maundy Thursday and Easter Day must have said to himself how very sorry he was. It needed an occasion in time and space when he could confess Christ in order to know and to receive that healing.

The environment and community of the faithful must be a place and must find a way for sinful men and women to reassert their will to love God and to confess Christ in faith while many of their deeds and words still betray him: 'To bind eternal truth' (their sonship through baptism) to 'present fact' (their frequent lapses of word and action, emotion and passion).

Confession in the Church today

All traditions of the Church need to find this expression if they are not to become either antinomian on the one hand or moralistic on the other. Dag Hammarskjold said he measured a man not by the number of his friends whom he kept round him but rather by the number of his critics whom he was able to keep about him. So the measure of catholic Christianity is not so much how many good people come to church but rather how many bad and mad people belong to the Christian community. But to good, bad and indiffer-ent Christians alike, the challenge is the same—renewal to holiness through repentance and forgiveness. In all traditions of the churches, the love of Christ should constrain us to continue a sacramental opportunity in a place and with a form by which ordinary men and

women can confess Jesus and hold together in a single piece their
eternal identity and their present failings so that they themselves may
become vehicles of his glory—people in whom heaven and earth are
striving for unity and reconciliation. The climate for this sacrament
is changing in the Roman Catholic Communion from a juridical and
formal act of confessing mortal sins in the presence of a priest to an
encounter under the judgement of the Gospel and in an environment
which is largely pastoral and open ended. For a rigid tradition, this
development should be only gain, but—and I think this is
important—there must still be sufficient flexibility even in a more
informal setting for ordinary people to be able to stammer out and
stutter the commonplace of ordinary human sins, without necessarily having to be conditioned by a largely middle-class practice
which resembles a cosy chat about spiritual things. In other words,
the pastor of sensitivity and ability will tailor this ministry to particular needs and particular circumstances—formal and informal—
without losing the precious and precise content of absolution formally stated and objectively expressed.

But no tradition can afford to ignore this pastoral application of
baptismal life, for to do so is to exchange the unique identity of
holiness for merely natural virtues, the wide sweep of catholicism for
the narrow clique of a religious ghetto. May I suggest a few particular and important pastoral considerations:

1 *Great expectations!*   The creation of the right expectations in the
life of a local church is set largely by the chief pastor in that place. His
preaching and teaching should lead naturally to a ministry of reconciliation. In old-fashioned Anglo-Catholicism the mission preacher
frequently spoke of 'preaching for first confessions'. In Biblical
Evangelical language, preaching evokes the response: 'What must I
do to be saved?' But all preaching and teaching from whatever
tradition should lead men and women to the next milestone in their
long Christian pilgrimage, and frequently such a milestone can be a
first confession, a return to the sacrament of reconciliation after
many years; or a special act of thanksgiving after illness; or after
many years of marriage; a birthday or anniversary of some kind—all
can be moments of deeper surrender to God in thankfulness for what

he has done. Corporately each year the congregation is to renew their baptismal vows at Easter in the liturgy, and this again is an opportunity to show what is once-for-all and yet what also needs to be frequently recalled with thankfulness at significant moments of growth and challenge. Linked with the 'laying-on-of-hands' and with prayer, the sacrament of reconciliation in the life of the congregation should be the way of growth in holiness and faith. Whether informally in the study (uninterrupted by telephones and without the expectation of small talk) or more formally in the setting of the church building, the pastor must be a minister of healing and reconciliation, never afraid to lead men and women to express their penitence and to reassert their will to love and serve God. This way of ministry is gospel-centred and is for ordinary men and women. We need desperately to recover this expectation in the ministry and life of the everydayChurch. The newly devised services of corporate penitence in the Roman Catholic Communion could most certainly be used to advantage by all Christians to help to create in a congregation this expectation of Christian penitence. It is this creation of the expectation that ordinary Christians are sinners and that sin is rather a matter-of-fact phenomenon in the Church that is so important in recovering both the catholicity and the holiness of the Church today. When I was a chaplain in London University a young man had made an appointment to see me and as he entered my room he looked so ill because he had just taken a hundred aspirin before arriving for his appointment! I rushed him round the corner to a nearby hospital to the casualty department and although at that moment I felt panic and a sense of drama, the moment we entered that casualty department we were surrounded by humanity with its many forms of everyday accident from a broken arm to a bad cut, from a burn to a road accident, and I shall never forget the words of the sister on duty as I rushed up to her to ask for some kind of priority treatment: 'Yes that's alright; just sit down and I'll be with you in a moment.' The Church is such a hospital where ordinary men and women in the distresses and accidents of life can present themselves for healing and wholeness, and at its best there is the same measure of that matter-of-fact acceptance in the medical profession as should pervade the pastoral ministry of reconciliation among those who are qualified and empowered to exercise such a ministry. The good priest is never shocked.

2 *Guilt or penitence*   Guilt is wounded pride: penitence is the response of lesser love to greater love. Penitence can come only after vision and insight and it is the work of God himself within us slowly revealing to us more and more of his love. Thank God we cannot see ourselves now as God sees us: the truth is spoken in love as we can best learn and receive it. 'Teach me as best my soul can bear' (Wesley).

'In thy light may we see light.' So through pastoral preaching, prayer and meditation and the reading of Scripture, we slowly see more and more of the features of Christ in their infinite beauty and unutterable love, and at each point we are prompted to true penitence. The first attitude in penitence is Godward and then only by implication do we look at our own shortcomings and turn in on ourselves. The classical shape of penitence is to be found in the sixth chapter of the book of the prophet Isaiah, verses 1–8: vision, penitence, forgiveness, vocation. The first step is always the same: 'Good God, *now* I see. It was always there, staring me in the face but *now* I see.' Such moments frequently bring us to our knees. We realise how blind we have been, but now it is as though scales fell from our eyes. 'Woe is me,' is the cry of Isaiah in an act of personal penitence in which he is conscious also of his corporate identity as a sinner. Isaiah confesses his sin. The gift of absolution is received and then he is able to hear and to see the way forward. 'Whom shall I send?' Life becomes vocation, not merely 'one damned thing after another'!

Only so is the life of God's people shaped and fashioned according to his will, and only so is the Church congregation rescued from that club mentality of belonging to such and such a church down the road. Only so is the Church prepared for its vocation to be God's people—'a people for his own possession'.

3 *More than counselling*   Of course counselling in some senses is part of the pastoral work of a priest and indeed of any pastor, and the confessional which degenerates into mere anonymous encounters with a few words gabbled by each party can become little more than magic. It is a sign of renewal in the Gospel in the Roman Catholic Communion that in the recent reforms the rather slick use 'of the box' has given way to a fuller expression of the sacrament in the fuller context of the gospel of reconciliation. It is frequently prefaced with an informal talk, the reading of Scripture and discussion involving both parties—the priest and penitent. But for other traditions who are reforming from an opposite end there is the problem that counselling could take the place of the actual declaration of forgiveness. Furthermore too much discussion can be rather a middle-class characteristic and the universality of this great sacrament can be lost if it degenerates into nothing more than a cosy chat, or a sophisticated discussion. At best the roles of priest and counsellor are quite distinct although they may overlap, and both should be available— not necessarily in the same agency.

For every person who can be helped by the open and informal encounter, there is at least another person who could be helped only by a more formal and more specific encounter in which the place and the form are clearly defined. The application of this sacrament and ministry today requires great flexibility, sensitivity and maturity by those who minister it, for what matters in the end is that God's people know how to seek reconciliation and can rejoice in the experience of God's great forgiveness and love. Perhaps we are permitted a slight parody of St Paul's phrase to drive this point home: 'You have many counsellors, but not many fathers in God!' (See 1 Corinthians 4:15.)

3. RENEWAL IN CATHOLICITY

For all men

If the vocation of the Church is to be 'in the world' but not 'of the world', then one of the challenges to the Church will be that it can never quite settle comfortably into the mould of the models which are in use in the thought of secular society. Of course the Incarnation demands that the Church should borrow and use both the models and the language of the world and of the age—to that extent the Church must be 'secular'. But the adage of Charles Williams always applies: 'This is thou: neither is this thou.' That is to say that the language and forms which are at hand and are of the age can reflect something of Christian life and expression, but sooner or later, they contradict the total content of the Gospel and its complete catholicity. In that sense the Church must be *in saecula saeculorum*. Our first impact with the world around us should be an affirmative one— 'yes': and then, sooner or later—'but'. There are plenty of Christians today who are all too ready to say to the world 'yes' and to be world affirming. Equally there is a reaction within the Christian Church itself into a dangerous fundamentalism which would be totally world denying and all too ready to say simply and finally—'no'. The fuller way of the Incarnation, the Crucifixion and the Resurrection, and the initiation into the ascended and glorified life even now on earth, is this more subtle approach summarised perhaps by the adage—'yes ... but'. We cannot reject the models and language, the forms and expressions of our world otherwise the Church has no roots and is failing to continue the work of the Incarnation. Part of the inevitable result of being an Incarnate Church is that to some extent it will be culturally conditioned. But equally if we are totally conformed to these models we shall fail to continue the work of re-ordering the world through the Cross and Resurrection, and the Church on earth will be detached from the fuller communion of the whole Church—in heaven and on earth. Worldly models will take us so far, but not far enough.

So with one of the models which is so often used for our understanding of the Church today. We speak of the Community of the Faithful. In an age of strong emphasis on community and communes, it is easy to see how the gathered Church can learn much from communities and groups which are such a strong characteristic of contemporary life. Yes, here is a useful model, but it does not go far enough and if we settle for it we will end up by contradicting the very nature of the catholicity of the Church. The mark—the distinctive mark—of the catholic Church and, ideally, of any one local congregation, is that it is a group of people who have nothing whatever in common except the one through whom they hold all things in common—Jesus Christ. The Christian Church is not simply a group of like-minded people—like liking like: that ends up in a kind of ecclesiastical freemasonry. We live at a time when the larger vision of the world is being fragmented into like-minded groups—the resurgence of tribalism and parochialism. Of course in a cold vast universe the natural tendency is to join in like-minded groups and the group and community expresses experiences that are very deep and full of meaning. Nevertheless, however deep and authentic are the experiences of the group, the mark of the catholic Christian congregation in any one area should be that it is the only place and the only group where such a cross-section finds true unity—that is the Communion of the Holy Spirit. In this sense the Church must be representative in its catholicity. How seldom does a bishop as he goes round his diocese and looks at the cross-section of the congregations, feel that this is the one group in this village or community which is truly representative.

Esprit de corps or even group consciousness is good but not good enough and the Communion of the Holy Spirit must cut right across such natural groupings if it is to represent the true nature of catholicity. The sacramental expression of such a reformed group is the Holy Communion—the sacrament of unity. Because house groups and other groups are strong in the life of the Church today and because they really do experience a very strong sense of fellowship, there is much talk about 'lay-celebration'. If the question is put in a certain way the answer seems logical and natural enough. 'Here is a group who have been meeting regularly and who have experienced a deep sense of local fellowship: why cannot one of them act as the natural president of that group rather than inviting an 'outsider' to celebrate simply because he is a priest?' Put that way of course the question is loaded and the answer is obvious. If, however, we stop to realise the limitations of any group—especially one which gets on so well together, or which has been through so much together—then we shall realise that much of its 'togetherness' comes from its exclusiveness: every club has its own club rules, and groups are no exception even if they meet in the name of Christ. Of course they can have a meal together—a community meal—in which there is a sense of corporate expression, but, however strong and authentic that expression may be, by very definition it cannot make the statement which the Holy Communion service is intended to make.

The Holy Communion is intended to make a double statement— to endorse and express the existing fellowship of a group, but also to cut across that dimension with the wider claims of catholicity, by making that group at one with the universal fellowship (*koinonia*) of the Holy Spirit: preserving the 'unity of the Spirit in the bond of peace'. Whatever else a 'group celebration' may be, it is not this total exercise unless it is united to the worldwide episcopate through the local representative—the priest. It is precisely because he is 'brought in' from 'outside' that the celebration is rescued from being just a local and indigenous event and launched into the wider statement of the unity of the universal Eucharist. For the priest as a sign of unity (and the Eucharist as a celebration of unity) has to face both ways— representing the local group to the whole Body of Christ, and the Body of Christ to the group. Only so can the group really partake of the Body of Christ (unless it is just to devour itself, as groups frequently do!). Only so can it be 'valid'—to use rather old-fashioned language.

For, the whole point of the apostolic ministry is that it is never merely indigenous—it belongs to the wider fellowship of which the bishop is the sign and that sign is the sign of catholicism—universalism—the Fellowship of the Spirit which is both local and indigenous but also universal and apostolic: which is comfortably immediate and yet which speaks disturbingly of other worlds and of more distant horizons: gathered in one place—yet scattered over the face of the earth: local, informal and vernacular, yet eternal and sharing in a unity which here on earth is still a mystery since it is the unity which exists at the very heart of the diversity of the Trinitarian Godhead. No, it is not just enough to see the Church as a group or a community. It is an Ecclesia—a group like nothing else on earth!

The total man
If catholic Christianity is essentially a statement about the unity of all mankind it is also intended to be a statement about the unity of the whole man, individually as well as corporately. The appeal of the Gospel is essentially addressed to the total man and not merely to any one aspect of his personality.

In the English-speaking expression of Christianity this issue revolves around a question of semantics. 'Flesh' versus 'spirit' is largely interpreted as things to do with the body (sexuality, food, drink, money) versus 'spiritual' which is here interpreted as an abstraction six feet above the earth, largely belonging to cloud-cuckoo land, unable to be tested in the hard world of economics, science and the laboratory. Such an antithesis rolls the pitch for the English game of Puritanism in which everything which speaks to the motives and passions of men is suppressed or indulged (depending upon the mood of the day or the day of the week) and everything which is aesthetic, impractical and pious is kept in a totally separate compartment and labelled 'spiritual'—only to be brought out on Sundays or when the vicar is invited to tea!

The New Testament is not aware of this sort of antithesis. The warfare in the New Testament is of quite a different kind and involves two totally different armies. In the New Testament, life lived 'in the flesh' is every aspect of life lived contrary to any reference to God, and strangely enough what so often parades as Church and spiritual life can still be very fleshly—turned away from God for his own sake and used simply for our needs and pleasures. I have frequently felt there is something very 'fleshly' about many prayer groups but if you were to suggest this to the pious participants they would be greatly shocked: they would protest wholly 'spiritual' motivation!

So St Paul can plead the need for a 'spiritual body', for in his language and thought the spiritual life was the whole of life (body, mind and spirit) lived under the direction and purpose of God. By the 'spiritual life' Paul would mean a godly life, centred upon God's purposes for the world: a deep and godly compassion for all who were in the world: a godly curiosity and spirit of adventure to explore the universe and to co-operate with God in Christ in the Redemption and fulfilment of that universe. A man does not become godly by turning his eyes to heaven but rather when he becomes 'God's spy' through a microscope or a telescope, deeply interested in and concerned with the world and in seeking to make that world a true reflection of the image of God.

So the appeal of catholic Christianity is not just to the pious few nor is it just an address to the spiritual side of man. The friends of Jesus have been a pretty motley crew and the lovely characteristic of sanctity is that it is never predictable: you tumble over it in the most unlikely places. There is always an element of surprise and of the unexpected about the work of grace upon nature. Heaven and earth are full of his glory if only we had eyes to see and ears to hear. The schizoid outlook of flesh versus spirit in this wrong sense is right at the heart of this English-speaking culture and little wonder that if the appeal of the Church is only to part of a man it should be able to speak only to part of mankind.

For if it is glory with which we are concerned (and many new religions might want to borrow that word) then we need to know that there is nothing unsubstantial or immaterial about this word, rightly understood. It is a difficult word to grasp in the Bible, for like all the best words it ends up by grasping you! In the Hebrew Bible the word that signifies glory, *kabod*, implies the idea of weight. So Paul speaks of 'the weight of glory'. Glory gives to the world a true significance: the candy floss of so much of our daily life, when it is lived in the Spirit to the full, becomes the substantial life which in the end literally 'carries weight'. It is a strange reversal: for it is the fleshly life, lived without glory, which is lightweight and unsubstantial, ephemeral and passing: it is the spiritual life which is substantial and carries weight. In the end we shall find that the spiritual world (properly understood) is made of rougher and tougher fibre than the world of the flesh, which even a puff of wind, let alone a storm, annihilates (see St Matthew 7:27).

If flesh versus spirit is one fragmentation in our world, then perhaps a more serious dichotomy is between head and heart. Of course the Christian religion by virtue of the Incarnation invades history and is not ashamed of the vocabulary of the philosopher. It has challenged and teased some of the greatest intellects in the world and whatever else the Christian religion may be it is never blatantly irrational. Nevertheless Chesterton's statement, already quoted, still stands: 'The madman is not the man who has lost his reason, but the man who has lost everything except his reason.'

Perhaps this madness is best seen in our attitude towards theology and to those who make theology. Theology and theologians in the recent Protestant and reformed traditions have become located almost exclusively in universities. Theology has been seen as primarily an intellectual exercise best pursued in the environment of the lecture theatre, the library and 'top-table' by those who are most at home in such an atmosphere. This is a new and recent emphasis. A vast quantity of theology has been written in the past by bishops, priests and country pastors, monks and lay men and women in the total environment of the life and worship, prayer and power of the Church.

'Theology is an encounter with the living God, not an uncommitted academic exercise. This encounter cannot survive if its only locus is the lecture theatre or the library' (Kenneth Leech: *Soul Friend*). Theology is an activity of the total person, and it is the activity of the whole Body of Christ. It is in the context of Christian experience and worship that theology comes alive. Equally an environment based solely upon experience, tradition and worship which is lacking the thrust of theology degenerates into a cult. If only the doors between the environment of the 'caps' and the 'mitres' could be flung open from both sides, theology would bring the Church a new prophetic thrust which is just as badly needed in the affluence of the West, as in South America and the Third World, where theology has been so powerful in recent years in arming the Church for its task of proclaiming the Gospel.

For theology at its best has frequently been 'occasional' theology responding to the events of the day in politics and the crises of war and prison camps. Such theology speaks to the total man and reflects this total encounter of a life lived theologically. Such a life speaks to the mind of course but not only to the cold analytical mind. St Augustine writes:

> Give me a man in love: he knows what I mean. Give me one who yearns; give me one who is hungry; give me one far away in this desert who is thirsty and sighs for the spring of the eternal country. Give me that sort of man: he knows what I mean but if I speak to a cold man he does not know what I am talking about.... (*Tract* in Joh. 4)

Here Augustine does not mean an irrational man nor simply a sensual man but a man who is super-rational. Unamuno writes: 'There are people who appear to think only with the brain or with whatever may be the specific thinking organ; while others think with all the body and all the soul, with the blood, with the marrow of the bones, with the belly, with the life' (Miguel de Unamuno *The Tragic Sense of Life* London 1962, page 33). That is the nature of the appeal and impact of catholic theology. The disease in the West since the secularisation of universities is a severe and destructive one for it has ceased to create a theology which makes its appeal to the total man. Newman saw the danger of this in his reflections upon the decline of teaching of theology in universities. He writes:

> I say then that if the various branches of knowledge, which are

the matter of teaching in the university, so hang together, that none can be neglected without prejudice to the perfection of the rest, and if theology be a branch of knowledge, of wide reception, of philosophical structure, of unutterable importance, and of supreme influence, to what conclusion are we brought from these two premises but this? That to withdraw theology from the public schools is to impair the completeness and invalidate the trustworthiness of all that is actually taught in them. I have urged that, supposing theology be not taught, its province will not simply be neglected, but will actually be usurped by other sciences, which will teach, without warrant, conclusions of their own in a subject matter which needs its own proper principles for its due formation and disposition. (*The Idea of a University*)

The tyranny of one form of intellectual discipline today has invaded the methodology of theology, and little wonder that theology has become the strange hybrid that we witness in much modern writing. For example we do not arrive at the Chalcedonian definition of the person of Christ by an analytical appeal solely to the pages of the New Testament—that is an inverted form of biblical fundamentalism. The Chalcedonian definition of the person of Christ is the outcome of the Church's reflection upon the person of Christ, in an environment of scripture, liturgy, repentance and the experience of forgiveness and healing in which the Bible and tradition are interwoven and interiorised. No department of theology can claim primacy in this process, and in the end the appeal is to the total man in his total experience of the redeeming work of Christ. This is not to say that the definition of Chalcedon is finished and packaged in a form which will be acceptable to every generation but what it does say is that any future development on this can never go back behind Chalcedon in the hope of finding a pure and demythologised definition of the person of Christ. We grow and we develop within the tradition of which the myth, the symbol and the story are part of the developing and living process. 'Wouldst thou plant for eternity? Plant then in the fantasy and in the inner recesses of the heart' (Thomas Carlyle). A Church which rejects the symbol and the fantasy will lose the ability to invade and irrigate the subconscious. It will become impotent in precisely that area in which its greatest power needs to be experienced. If its prayer and worship are merely straightforward, clinical and only cerebral it will become arid and intellectual, moralistic and serious. The genius of catholic spirituality is its ability to speak to head and heart and to bring the two together: 'stand before God with your head in your heart,' says Bishop Theophan. That is always the posture of the whole man in the presence of his God. The old antithesis between head and heart, between intellect and intuition must be transcended. The only thing worse than a hearty religion is the heady religion of the iconoclast. Of course all icons have a strange knack of becoming idols and we cover them with all kinds of layers of self-glory which in the end rob them of their ability to point beyond themselves to glorify the one who is always beyond all our images and our wildest imaginings. However, if we try to have no images or icons or worse still if we make them appeal only to the intellect, then beware! We shall exchange the comparatively harmless icons of our childhood for the sophisticated icons of our manhood. An intellectual icon is far more likely to turn into an idol. I am not half so much in danger of actually believing in a 'daddy-in-the-sky' as I am of being convinced by such a dangerous phrase as 'the ground of my being'. It is comparatively easy to discard the naïvety of the former image when it no longer helps, but it is not so easy to sit lightly to the latter image. We are in far greater danger of being seduced into idolatry by this image, not least because it can claim such a distinguished pedigree in the history of its usage (see Julian of Norwich). Of course, the truth is that all images can be helpful and some more than others for some people, sometimes. The 'ground of my being' is for many people not just jargon, but has led to a revolution in their way of thinking about God and of learning to pray. But if we merely swap one image for another—albeit a more 'sophisticated' image—we are still in danger of idolatry, unless we can live with the contradiction of Charles Williams at the heart of all our comprehension and contemplation: 'This is thou: neither is this thou.'

We need to recover the basic symbols of the Scriptures and to uncover them and permit them to be the powerful images and effective symbols which alone can speak to 'the deepest of all experiences of the deepest of all facts' (von Hügel). As a bishop who frequently has to baptise from a 'portable font' the size of an egg-cup, I yearn to recover the powerful image of drowning in a baptistry which is worthy of the name. I always think that the tidy sacristan is to blame to a large extent for the decadence of liturgical symbolism! Drowning is a messy process; breaking bread leaves lots of 'fragments to be gathered up': oil is best kept in kitchens or garages, and as for fire—well it is positively dangerous. (The coalition of Church furnishing companies and tidy sacristans has a lot to answer for!)

The symbol of the body
The basic symbol of the New Testament throughout the teaching of Christ and the Gospels and in the experience and theology of St Paul and St John is the symbol of the body. The New Testament is littered with body language and yet in the history of the Church there have only been comparatively few moments when this deafening symbol has really attracted the attention that it deserves. True health is a total response of the total person in which all the processes of mind, intuition, and passion are brought to bear and in which the hands and the body play no small part. If an individual is to be healthy and to cohere, this total process is something which speaks to his total person, but an age of specialisation has brought about its own particular alienations and disintegrations. In place of routine and regularity, by which aspects of the whole person are brought to bear upon daily work, hobbies and everyday life, we now have specialisation by which small parts of ourselves are used and employed to the exclusion of our total self. It is, of course, true that many compensate for this specialisation in their work by diversification in their hobbies and other interests. Frequently the mathematician is also the organist or makes model railway engines as his hobby; equally in large industrial cities in the past it was the manual worker who kept pigeons, went fishing or had his allotment for gardening, so employing the intuitive side of his nature in his hobbies.

But the age of specialisation has brought a deep alienation. We have 'educated' people to lose everything except their heads: bodies without heads might be ghosts: but heads without bodies are madmen. It is that kind of madness and sickness which is at the heart of our society both in its education and in its daily employment and life. The heady demands of big industry and increasing specialisation bring their own compensation as more and more people become 'out of touch' with their bodies, their roots and the earth.

'The head cannot say to the hands "I have no need of you." Neither can the feet say to the eye "I have no need of you." ' This image of St Paul in his first Epistle to the Corinthians is indeed a prescription not only for the health of the individual body but should be employed in the wider imagery and symbolism of the Body of the Church and indeed of society at large.

If the words of St Paul are true of the individual body how much more they are true of the body of society. Here the alienation begins to pick up and carry overtones of politics and class distinction. If educational ethos again and again implies that machines work while only men think: that the manual and the mental processes are in such contrast, then sooner or later, the sickness of the individual body in society will spill over into a sickness of the body politic. In place of a true interdependence there will grow the attitude of an unhealthy rivalry and eventually blackmail and exploitation. 'The head cannot say to the hands "I have no need of you." ' Compete rather than complete will be the slogan of this outlook.

It was St Benedict who found in his Rule of Life the healthy place for manual work so that his monks employed every side of their personality to grow into a harmonious whole.

St Benedict prescribed that 'manual labour' and 'sacred reading' should alternate in the daily rhythm of the monastery. To this end times for each were carefully determined, but 'manual labour', far from being regarded as inferior to intellectual pursuits, is raised by Benedict to a status which sees it as truly part of the life and work of the apostle: 'then are they truly monks when they live by the labour of their hands, like our fathers and the apostles' (*Rule of St Benedict* Chapter 48).

Some theologians and historians would actually blame the Protestant work ethic for that ethos which has plagued the West whereby work has become dirty. Dirty work—the tilling of the earth—was seen to be a direct result of the Fall of Man and therefore in some sense to be 'risen above'. This is, of course, in sharp contrast to the catholicism of the Middle Ages. Augustine was to say: 'To work is to pray: to pray is to work.' In that dictum he held together what only later became opposite ends of the pole. Of course the hard lines of specialisation had yet to be drawn and few were far from the earth and death in the medieval scene when a horse was a means of transport and food was unpackaged. Hands and heads were daily in co-operation and neither carried the tags of inferiority or superiority. The university—as the name suggested, was an education for the whole man and not an island of specialisation.

Whatever the historical causes of our present sad alienation may be, its reality is with us. Little wonder that we exploit all that is in the earth while seeking to grow ever farther away from it into the towers of glass and concrete where the only touch we exercise is the touch of a button or a switch. Our interior enmity of hand versus head is externalised into the enmity between classes within industry and in society at large. The parody of St Paul becomes a slogan for hostility and strife. In fact the head says daily to the hand 'I can manage without you,' while the hand says to the head: 'Now, let's see if you can get by without me!'

Of course we see all kinds of tokenism at work from the resurgence of Yoga to the buying of country cottages, where the 'simple things' of life can be reclaimed, rediscovered and enjoyed. It must be admitted that such options are open only to one small sector of our society for obvious economic reasons, while it is much more difficult for the manual worker without even a small back-yard or allotment and perched on the nineteenth floor of a block of flats, to have even tokens of other outlets for other sides of his personality.

The founder of the Christian Church left us not so much a bundle of ideas about a good life, but rather he gave us his Body. St Paul is not afraid to take this deafening symbol and to listen most carefully to all it is saying throughout the whole of his theology. The society of the Church was to be for him like a body in which the head could not exploit other parts and yet in which all parts of the body had a deep interdependence if they were to play their part in an ordered and healthy fashion. All specialisation within this image is to be built upon a deep interdependence of all the parts, for only this would

bring about the health of the whole body individually or corporately.

Furthermore, for St Paul, 'headship' does not imply domination.
This is especially important when he applies the imagery of the body
to the relation between the Persons of the Trinity and also the
relationship between men and women. 'The head of every person is
Christ, the head of a woman is her husband and the head of Christ is
God' (1 Corinthians 11:3). Man is no more superior to woman in this
statement, than the Father is superior to the Son. There is true
equality, without interchangeability. There is true equality because
of a relationship of interdependence and the unity of a single will.
That is the reconciliation which the Gospel intends between the head
and the body, intellectual and manual, heaven and earth, man and
woman. This sort of theological image is intended by Paul to carry
enormous weight and is deliberately heavily charged with social and
political overtones.

Christ feeds us with his body in order that we may become his
body for, as Feuerbach commented more accurately than he could
ever have supposed: 'Man is what he eats.' Jesus in St John's Gospel
Chapter six presses this analogy to its ultimate—cannibalism. He is
in effect saying that we cannot have a purely spiritual relationship
with God which by-passes Christ. God and man were alienated at
that level in our former nature through the Fall. Now man can recover union with God only through Christ: the Incarnate Christ,
flesh of our flesh and bone of our bone. Our union with Christ must
be an incarnate union through those very elements in which Christ is
clothed by the nature of his Incarnation—flesh and blood and water.
There are many today who still wish to spiritualise union with God
or union with Christ and are as outraged by the literalism of the
implications of the Incarnation as those who listened to Christ in St
John's Gospel Chapter six, and who subsequently no longer 'walked
with him'. The universal claim of catholic Christianity is as earthed
as this. There is no ascension into heaven unless there has first been a
descending into the lower parts of the earth. 'Now the word
"ascended" implies that he also descended to the lowest level, down
to the very earth. He who descended is no other than he who
ascended far above all heavens, so that he might fill the universe'

(Ephesians 4:9–10). Glory for the Christian is earthed and rooted in a body. At this stage our 'fleshly body' is already an anachronism as we wait for the final fulfilment of the Christian life in that 'spiritual body' which will be even more full and more permanent and capable of many more dimensions than this body.

I really do believe that the 'spiritual body' for which we wait and yearn will express all the unfulfilled desires of this body of the earth: promiscuity and the desire to be in more places than one at once, when they are redeemed from selfishness and pride, may yet well be seen to be not such unheavenly desires, after all! We may be talking about little more than what it must be like to be a butterfly from the point of view of a caterpillar. Thank God we shall not be drifting spirits but we shall be embodied persons with a reality which is even firmer and made of sterner stuff than the so-called real world of flesh and blood in which we live.

The dangers of spiritualising

The Christian faith of course does not just come true naturally, and there are many 'stumbling blocks' along the route, but perhaps the stumbling block to our contemporary world, which is compara-tively ready to swallow 'religion', is the stumbling block of the religion of the Incarnation. Although religion and 'things of the spirit' have a new vogue, there is a sense in which a religion which is rooted in the 'here-and-now' will never be in vogue: it is uncomfort-ably relevant and demandingly immediate. It is always much more convenient to have a religion which is literally six feet above contra-diction, imprisoned in a 'spiritual dimension' and unable to invade and challenge the world of flesh and blood reality. Gnosticism (for that is the umbrella name for such spiritual religions) is always hovering around uncomfortably close to catholic Christianity as a preferable perversion and the more comfortable alternative.

There are other reasons today, however, which encourage the climate of spiritualising and Gnosticism. Since Descartes, philoso-phy in the Western world has found no place for the metaphysic. The medieval synthesis, through its philosophy and its poetry, through its maps and its world-view, was able to hold together in a single whole the world of matter and of spirit. The theology of the reformers was a response to the break-up of this synthesis, and it created a schizoid world-view from which neither Christianity nor our culture has recovered to this day. Luther in his debate with Zwingli in the *Schloss* at Marburg said that if Zwingli's world-view prevailed it would lead to a loss of 'that unity of word and deed, of picture and thing, of the bread and the glorified body—body will become merely body and symbol merely symbol'. Although Luther won the debate, Zwingli has won the day, and we suffer in our present world from precisely the dichotomy that Luther sensed. For Luther was still sufficiently the medieval monk, nurtured in the warm climate of the medieval synthesis, to sense the strong and cold winds that were blowing from northern Europe in the name of Renaissance and Reformation. But for the Western world since the sixteenth century there has been a splintering of our world-view, until 'body has become merely body' and 'symbol merely symbol'. This makes the task of the apologist for a religion of Incarnation extremely difficult, and indeed it is probably true to say that until there is a break-through in our understanding of matter (possibly from the side of the physicist) or our way of expressing our experiences (possibly from the side of the philosopher or even the psychologist) there will be no strategic break-through for the religion of the Incarnation. Archbishop Anthony Bloom addressing hospital chaplains, doctors and nurses in a symposium says these words:

I think that it is terribly important that all our Churches should rethink the problems of matter, of the Incarnation, of the Sacraments, of miracles, against that kind of background, because what makes our theology so hopelessly inadequate is that we all implicitly or explicitly accept the material world on the terms of the materialist and, having accepted the material world in that way, we then put on top of it, or push into it, things like Incarnation, the change of bread and wine to the Body and Blood of Christ, the miracles, and so on. We then have to work out two kinds of theology. It is either a magic theology, or a theology that makes nonsense of what we say. When we say, for instance, 'in a spiritual manner', we usually mean 'I don't believe it, but I say it';

because we do not make friends 'in a spiritual manner'; we do not
eat our lunch 'in a spiritual manner'. We do things in a 'spiritual
manner' only when we want to keep the word safe from our
complete disbelief in the event. We will never solve this problem
unless we have an adequate theology of things material and then
we can, as doctors, nurses, chaplains and so on, think of the
bodies of people whom we treat in quite new terms, in terms that
begin with the seed sewn in corruption and ending with the
Transfiguration and the Ascension and the 'sitting at the right
hand of the Father'. (*From Fear to Faith—Studies of Suffering and
Wholeness*, Ed. Norman Autton, SPCK 1971)

But the truth is that many Christians still insist on speaking 'in a
spiritual manner' and this dichotomy between matter and spirit,
heaven and earth, persists and pervades the spirituality and any
commitment to the social gospel in most of the Churches today. For
the Christian 'spy' is not a man looking for a different world, but a
man who looks at the world very differently. Flesh and blood, bricks
and mortar, bread and wine, and every blade of grass are 'full of his
glory' and are potentially reaching out to bear the glory and image of
Christ as surely as the Virgin Mary bore him in her womb. Such a
world-view and vision could lead C. S. Lewis to write:

There are no *ordinary* people. You have never talked to a mere
mortal. Nations, cultures, arts, civilisations—these are mortal,
and their life is to ours as the life of a gnat. But it is immortals
whom we joke with, work with, marry, snub and exploit—
immortal horrors or everlasting splendours. This does not mean
that we are perpetually solemn. We must play. But our merriment must be of that kind (and it is in fact the merriest kind) which
exists between people who have, from the outset, taken each
other seriously—no flippancy, no superiority, no presumption.
And our charity must be a real and costly love with deep feeling
for the sins in spite of which we love the sinner—no mere toler-
ance, or indulgence which parodies love as flippancy parodies
merriment. Next to the Blessed Sacrament itself, your neighbour

is the holiest object presented to your senses. (*They asked for a Paper* C. S. Lewis)

Particularity and universality

But such a world-view must not be afraid of particularities. It must be prepared to speak of somewhere and not merely everywhere or anywhere: someone and not merely everyone or anyone: something and not merely everything or anything. God is everywhere, but I can only come to know him somewhere because he is infinite and I am finite. If I try to know him everywhere I shall probably end up knowing him nowhere and yet if I wish to know him everywhere I must start by knowing him somewhere. If I try to arrive at universalism in one step I shall end up knowing God nowhere and worse still I shall end up endorsing the fantasy that I am infinite and God is finite. We do not grow in love by trying to love everyone, but rather by learning to love someone: set out trying to love everyone and you'll end up loving nobody. Anyone can fall in love with love—just try marrying the brute!

The price of the Incarnation was precisely that the God who is everywhere could only present himself to our senses by becoming a man somewhere. It is important to note that he became a man and not mere humanity and part of the limitations of the Incarnation are rooted in the fact that to become part of our humanity offered only two choices. He became a man in order to relate to everyone by a re-ordering and restructuring of all our relationships through mutual interdependence and complementality. If he had become an hermaphrodite he would have been related to no one! He would merely have created another world and another problem. He could not become a universal man, he had to become a Jew, for once again, if he had created another category of no nationality, it would have been no help to the world at all. The way to universality is always in this world *through* particularity, and at the outset it seems inevitably like a reduction and a denial of the general and the more generous vision. At the outset and with foresight the affirmation of everything seems to demand the laying aside of something—it is the eye of the needle, and 'rich men' reluctant to let go of possessions find it difficult to go through this process in order to keep all their possessions. The modern intellectual man finds this a hard nettle to grasp: he wants to stand back and take up what initially seems a more universalist and generous position. For him, God (if he exists) must be everywhere in general and nowhere in particular: divine acts of consecration (if such be possible) belong to all times in general and no time in particular. There is a paralysis of intellectual analysis which would lead you never actually on the one hand to consecrate bread and wine or on the other hand even to sign a cheque!

Such a view may spring from fear of commitment—for frequently the cerebral intellectual is a sort of 'voyeur' preferring to look at, or write poetry about, the event rather than actually to pick the fruit. Of course, it may simply be due to the inevitable result of trying to play God, just a piece of old-fashioned egotism in which I refuse to be simply a creature taking up my place in Creation in a right relationship to my Creator.

Nevertheless the claim of catholic Christianity rests upon this universality through particularity in which the route to heaven is through the earth of which God in Christ has become part. 'There is a communion with God, there is a communion with the earth; there is a communion with God through the earth' (Teilhard de Chardin). We lost both of the first of these two relationships through the Fall when we were alienated both from our roots and from our goal. Enmity is at our feet and at our heads. We are without roots and without a goal and in that sense fallen man is indeed 'cut off from the land of the living'. The only way left to us is through 'a communion with God *through* the earth'—and it is through our baptism into Christ that we first descend in order to re-ascend and to fill all things—man as the mediator in turn through whom the whole Creation is brought back into communion with God in Christ. Man redeemed must reclaim and gather up the fragments that remain because nothing is lost. Man in this sense must once again have feet of clay—that is his glory: leave wings to angels (that is their glory presumably!).

And so, for the religion of the Incarnation there is continuity and discontinuity: Creation and Redemption belong together. The slow consecration of the universe is the work of the Church and the end product is the kingdom in which God's rule is re-established in man and for man. But there is that *double* action—'in man and for man'. What Christ experienced was in man and for man. He was most representative by being most particular. There was no solution to the problem if it were held six inches away in a clinical and detached way. Christ was in man and so he was for man: his desire to be for man compelled him to enter into man.

A godless age which has fractured into a false individualism inevitably loses any sense of the solidarity of mankind in its fight against totalitarianism. It may be that this is a healthy and inevitable battle for survival as an individual in a world of generalities and false universalism. But such an age also loses any sense of the representative figure. As ever-larger committees and bodies, we strive to be 'representative', but before long such a view of democracy becomes so unwieldy as to be the very best preparation for the short cuts of tyranny. At the heart of Christianity is the doctrine of representation. In Isaiah the Servant is a representative figure who points to the vocation of Israel as being essentially representative—'for the sake of all nations'. Paul takes his whole stand for redemptive theology upon the solidarity of mankind in sin as well as in salvation; the representative nature of Adam as well as the new Adam; and in his doctrine of marriage he goes even further—representative becomes vicarious as the unbelieving wife 'is sanctified by the believing husband' (1 Corinthians 7:14). In the fourth Gospel Christ sees as the highest sign of sacrificial love that vicarious quality of life: 'Greater love hath no man than this that a man lay down his life for his friends' (St John 15:13). These are not simply the words for an epitaph: it is not simply a way of dying; it is a way of living. Life in the kingdom will be vicarious so the Church which points to the kingdom is a body in which if 'one suffers all suffer and if one is glorified all are glorified' (1 Corinthians 12:26).

So with the catholic Church. It must see itself as representative and vicarious. William Temple could write: 'The Church is the one club which exists for the sake of those who are not members of it.' It is not only for the sake of those who are not in the Church that the Christian sanctifies himself but also for the sake of the whole Creation which 'eagerly awaits' our adoption; for without us it cannot enter upon its glory. In this sense man is the priestly figure in the whole process of Redemption and therefore the essential character and nature of the Church is a priestly one: the priesthood of all believers. (It is worth pointing out perhaps that the priesthood of all believers is not the same thing as the priesthood of every believer, and that here again we shall not understand the relationship between the ordained ministry and all the other ministries of the Church unless we seize hold upon this category of the representative figure. A priest is for the Church what the Church is for the world.) The scriptural economy is adamant and consistent throughout Old and New Testaments alike: the many are saved by the few: the few are saved by the one. Yet if the remnant is not to become just an oddment it must see its vocation in these larger terms of representative and vicarious, entering upon the labours of Christ in order that others may enter upon our labours. This chain of glory is a mystery indeed, in which even little ones must not be despised, in which the blood of the martyrs is the seed of the Church; in which the majority is not the all-conclusive factor and in which there was a time when it did not seem excessively absurd for some to be baptised on behalf of the dead. This is a world-view which, once it is laid hold upon, has a secret which indeed unlocks the universal door which all men yearn to open. But this world-view is not easily held at the present time and members of the fellowship of the Incarnation need to be re-schooled if they are to grasp this vision and not merely to concede the current patterns of thought of the secular world which will undermine totally any doctrine of the catholicity of the Church. Nevertheless this is the stuff of the saints and rightly recovered is the seed of renewal in catholicism.

Pastoral reflections and applications for today

The recovery by the churches of a fuller and richer understanding of the nature of catholicity is crucial to the renewal of Christianity in our contemporary world. As we have seen, this must imply to some extent standing over and against the current of much contemporary thought. This, however, must not be done in the spirit of a 'citadel mentality', resistant to all influences and yearnings within our so-

RENEWAL IN CATHOLICITY   83

ciety, but rather in a spirit of contributing to our world such insights as we have from our faith which are precious and rich, and so bringing to the world a deeper and fuller vision of life and the potential of the world in which we live. For in the end catholicism is truly world-affirming. Those who have been most committed to its teaching have been most committed to the world in which they have lived and have contributed most generously to the formation of its society and its culture.

1 *A right use of God's world*   For too long the Calvinistic world-view of the total depravity of Creation has invaded Christianity and in its turn has rubbed off on the much wider popular opinion about the world and matter and things of the earth. Little wonder that in the West—in the English-speaking West in particular—there has been such gross exploitation of the environment and of the resources of the earth. The opposite of a false spiritualism is an aggressive materialism, and unless we can challenge such a false spiritualism with a genuine sacramentalism there is no way in which the earth and its resources can be truly cherished and rightly used: the 'world as sacrament'. A false spiritualism which abandons any concern for matter and the world will leave the latter to the blatant materialist. It is only the sacramentalist who can build a bridge between the ideals of true spirituality and the higher pragmatism of a genuine concern for the things of this world. The catholic Christian must have a love of the world—the created order—and seize it as the raw material of glory when it is rightly used and directed according to the will and purposes of God. In the English translation of the New Testament once again we have a problem of semantics with the use of the word 'world'. Two Greek words give us a single English word. The created order is loved by God: 'God so loved the world' (St John 3:16). The world that we are commanded to hate is 'the passing age' and its fads and fancies, but both the gospel-accounts, and, above all, the attitude of Jesus demand that we should love the created order and give thanks for it at 'all times and in all places'. The Eucharist is itself a declaration of a right love of the created order and should ideally be both a manifesto and a slogan for all who care about the environment as well as for those who are impelled to social action and the love and care of neighbour. For such a sacramental view of the world there is no antithesis between the worship of God in the sacrament of the altar, a right use and distribution of the world resources, feeding of the poor and the housing of the homeless. For the sacramental Christian this represents one great sweep of compassion and love.

The Eastern Churches seem to be better at holding together their theology of Creation and Redemption. It may be that, because they are not so much influenced by Augustinian theology, they seem to have a theology of the sacraments which extends beyond a short list of specific sacraments and spills over into a whole list of sacramentals of which the icon is perhaps the most obvious. In the West the sacraments are a tightly defined category and tend to stop short by failing to lead the mind and vision from a commitment to something somewhere to that larger awareness of everything everywhere. In the East there is consecrated bread but there is also blessed bread. In the West the consecrated bread is locked away in a separate category for the adoration and love of the faithful but so often fails to be seen as food for the journey and strength for the truly Christian revolution of love and compassion.

It is a pity that the feast of the Transfiguration does not loom larger in the Western tradition than it does. Rightly seen it is the bridge between Incarnation and Crucifixion and Resurrection for it points in the New Testament account to the Exodus of the redemptive Christ. Maisie Spens in her amazing book *Receive the Joyfulness of your Glory* speaks of the Transfiguration as the feast of the conception of the Church. Seen as this it brings a right continuity between Creation and Redemption, clothing the Church itself in the very material and 'swaddling clothes' of natural life and so focusing a theology so gloriously summarised by Irenaeus: 'the glory of God is man come alive.' Redemption is seen not so much as rescuing man from the wickednesses of the Creation, but rather releasing him, and the whole created order through him, to become what it is intended by God to be: to release the potential of Creation so that it may enter the only environment in which it can truly flourish and not be frustrated—the environment of the life of the Blessed Trinity itself.

Social action, environmental stewardship and all political

involvement for the sacramental Christian spring not haphazardly from the chances of his own particular enthusiasms but inevitably from a vision of Creation as the work and concern of the same Person of the Trinity who is most deeply involved in Redemption. Rightly seen Creation, Redemption and sanctification are the single will and purpose of all three Persons of the Trinity and there is no antithesis between Creation and Redemption as there is no division between the Persons of the Trinity.

St Athanasius reminds us in his treatise *De Incarnatione verbi Dei*

The renewal of Creation has been wrought by the self-same Word who made it in the beginning. There is thus no inconsistency between Creation and Salvation; for the one Father has employed the same Agent for both works, effecting the salvation of the world through the self-same Word who made it at the first. (Chapter 1:1)

St John in the prologue to his Gospel is equally adamant—'all things were made by him (the Word) and without him was not anything made that was made' (St John 1:3). It is not possible to talk of the discontinuity between Creation and Redemption, nature and grace, natural theology and revealed theology until the continuity is first affirmed and appreciated. Perhaps the largest point of division between Catholics and Evangelicals in the Church of England is in precisely this area of theology for it carries many implications and practical applications in the everyday life of God's people, and perhaps this is an area where Catholics and Evangelicals need most to struggle to achieve a common understanding and a common mind.

2 *Christian formation*   The principles of a true understanding of catholicity also most certainly apply in the teaching and preaching work of the Church for the building up of Christian congregations and also for the training of the clergy. The dichotomy between head and heart, intellect and intuition and the slavish copying of methods of secular education in communicating the Gospel and in the training of the clergy, have created and endorsed a largely middle-class Christianity. Nothing that I say here is intended in any way to underestimate the vital importance of making a theological appeal to the intellect and indeed of the uttermost importance of an intellectual integrity in Christian apologetics. Nevertheless, the intellect must have neither more nor less importance than it deserves in Christian communication. The tyranny of the cerebral part of man's nature does not lead to maturity but rather deformity. It does not mean, however, the creating of mediocrity in all, but rather an excellence in all with each contributing his particular excellence to the whole in any total environment of learning. In Acts 2:42, apostolic doctrine is set in the fuller context of 'fellowship, breaking of bread, and prayer'. Such a curriculum is the concern of the whole body and not simply of intellectuals and can involve any local congregation in its entirety. Seen in this way the local congregation is the natural training unit of the Church. Liturgy, prayer and fellowship as well as Bible-study and doctrine are constituents within this total environment to which all have a contribution to make and from which all can take something for the building up of the total body.

It is this same environment which is ideally the one for the training of priests; and our theological colleges should be much more extensions of this kind of environment of learning, belonging to the total life of the Church, rather than pale reflections of modern universities and technical colleges on the one hand or monasteries on the other. In such a way theology could come alive for all God's people and also be formed in this total environment. A false theological specialisation has brought alienation from the body, and the end product of this breed of theology is unworthy of the name. Catholic renewal in the Churches will come only when we recover this richer and fuller sense of training and there is a renewal of theology itself. The split in the ranks of the clergy is terrifying between those who are good pastors and have given up even trying to read theology and those who find theology a compensation for a disastrous pastorate and who are subsequently farmed out to theological faculties or worse still put into positions of specialisation, ie teaching posts in theological colleges responsible for the training of future pastors and clergy or lay training departments and university chaplaincies.

The Institute of Christian Studies at Margaret Street in London, founded in 1970, fired the imagination of hundreds of lay people of many differing intellectual and other capabilities and showed to the Church another way of training in this fuller and richer understanding. Happily the idea has caught on not only in many Anglican churches but also most conspicuously at Westminster Cathedral. Ideally the schools of the Church should be formed around the bishop's chair, and the chief pastors of Christ's flock should themselves be conspicuous as the trainers and teachers of the Church. The bishop's household and its extension in the life and liturgy of the cathedral is the natural environment for the training of the diocese and, although specialisation will demand special courses and some specialists, there must be the pervading sense of belonging to the whole Church and being part of the 'household of faith' if theology is to be part of mainstream Christianity and not some strange aberration. In many ways the key to this is the episcopate itself—but more of that in the next chapter.

3 *The heart of the matter*   The heart of the matter is of course that Christian congregations large or small, should live and experience the fuller life of the risen and ascended Christ here on earth through the liturgy, in their prayers and in their fellowship. They all must be one with the fellowship of the saints. I want to make a very practical and pastoral suggestion. Lent has really got completely out of hand in the proportion and place it holds in the Christian calendar. The heart of the matter is the Three Days (*Triduum*)—Maundy Thursday, Good Friday, Holy Saturday. The liturgy of the Church in those three days encapsulates the whole Christian experience. It is the time of the renewal of the Church around the font, the newly baptised Christians and the renewal of baptismal vows by the whole of God's people. It is then that we celebrate the Risen Life—Resurrection, Eastertide, Rogationtide as preparation for the Ascension, and the asking for the gifts of the ascended Christ to equip God's people; Pentecost: Corpus Christi leading through to Petertide and the Ordination of the new priests.

It is not just flippant to say that those fifty days or so should be the time when clergy and laity alike come together with special diligence, starting with Holy Week and ending with summer holidays!

The weather (at least in the Western hemisphere) is better—it is the time of better health and more sunshine. The pastoral strategy of a parish should be geared to this period with courses and vigils, fasting and feasting rather than the wholly negative attitude of Lent only remotely connected with Easter, after which both clergy and laity alike generally disintegrate in exhaustion and defeat! All courses should be geared to these eight weeks from Palm Sunday to Trinity Sunday—and the liturgy of the Church should be the main environment in which all that is learned is both celebrated and interiorised. Lent Courses, influenza, strikes and fog are not the best environment for Christian formation. English religion has always focused around Ash Wednesday and Good Friday and it does not seem to have got us very far. Could we try Holy Saturday and Pentecost as two different antennae—well at least give it a chance!

4. RENEWAL IN APOSTOLICITY

Jesus the one and only Priest

The teaching of the New Testament and the consistent witness of the Church is that Jesus Christ is the one and only true Priest. It is the Epistle to the Hebrews which most clearly works out and makes explicit what is implicit throughout the pages of the New Testament on this matter. So the writer of the Epistle to the Hebrews baldly states that Jesus is 'High Priest of our Confession' (Hebrews 3:1). He is not just another priest sharing in the ministry and character of former lines of priesthood—he is unique and his priesthood is unique. It is the type of which all others are only the prototypes. 'He is not a High Priest who is unable to sympathise with our weaknesses, but one who in every respect was tempted as we are yet without sinning' (Hebrews 4:15). But the priesthood of Jesus is God's own declaration whereby he declares Jesus to be both his Son ('Thou art my Son, today have I begotten thee') and also a Priest ('Thou art a priest for ever after the order of Melchizedek'— Hebrews 5:5–6).

The writer to the Hebrews is intent on dragging into the discussion, in ways which at first seem tedious, the strange figure of Melchizedek from the pages of the Old Testament. Yet for the purposes of the argument as it is outlined in the Epistle to the Hebrews, Melchizedek is important because he is a striking symbol of the strange uniqueness of Christ precisely because he (Melchizedek) does not derive his priesthood from any other source, being 'without father or mother, or genealogy and has neither beginning of days nor end of life, but resembling the Son of God, he continues a priest for ever' (Hebrews 7:3). Melchizedek is a prototype of the priesthood of Jesus rather than the Levitical line which precedes Jesus as a Jew, and this is important to the writer of this Epistle precisely because the priesthood of Jesus is not derived but is God's own direct and unique gift, rooted back in the very act of Creation itself.

Jesus in this sense then is the end of all priesthoods. He is not just a priest among priests. He does not take his place in a line of priests nor is he a member of a caste of priests as in the case of the Levitical priesthood. So Melchizedek is a useful prototype to convince the reader of the uniqueness of Christ's priesthood. Furthermore, that priesthood is rooted in the moral commitment of Christ in obedience to his Father, therefore his priesthood is apostolic by its very nature. After Christ's baptism he is 'driven out' (ἐκβαλλειν) by the Holy Spirit for his life of combat with evil, and his confrontation with darkness, his Passion and Crucifixion. In all of this God the Father was totally involved for he was 'in Christ reconciling the world to himself'. Christ's life, death and Resurrection are the events in which he is united to mankind and to God and only so can he reconcile the two. However we may express the formula of christology we must equally involve both parties if we are to speak about reconciliation in any full sense of the word. It is the work of reconciliation which makes Christ the one kind of priest that mankind has needed from the dawn of history and of which every other kind of priesthood is a shadow and pale image, intuitively feeling out and reaching forward to the unique priesthood of our salvation, even Jesus Christ.

The Bible speaks of the human race as alienated from God and separated desperately from him and therefore divided within itself since humanity has lost the point of focus and reference through which alone it can achieve true unity and peace. Such a situation calls for a priest, and the main stream of Christian belief has never been ashamed to insist on the need for a mediator uniting God to man in his own person, in his actions, in his life, his death and inevitably in sacrifice. This is the motive and the power of that apostolicity of

Christ which compels him to set out upon his priestly pilgrimage 'despising the Cross for the joy that was set before him'. Dr Robert Terwilliger in his essay on priesthood writes:

In times of relative prosperity and peace, like the past few years, Christians get self-satisfied about human nature and dangerously optimistic about man. There are signs of this naïve unrealism now going away in the presence of an uncertain future. Nevertheless it is easy to lose the sense of our need of deliverance, and even come to think of salvation as nothing more than therapy. One consequence of this is to think of priesthood in purely human and functional terms. The priest is regarded as just a person who is chosen by the religious community to represent 'the community' to God and God to 'the community'. He is recognised, perhaps, because of his gifts and competence, and set apart by some official act to do this professionally. In his person he gathers 'the community' symbolically to himself in the offering of prayer and sacrifice to God, and speaks and acts on behalf of God towards them all. There is no such concept in the New Testament. To put it bluntly, it is a different religion.

There is only one priest Jesus Christ. He and he alone can bond God and man because of what he is as the Incarnate Unity of God and man. This essential Christian perception is movingly expressed in the eucharistic hymn of William Bright:
  'Look, Father, look, on his annointed face;
  And only look on us as found in him.' (The Rt Revd Dr Robert E. Terwilliger *Ordination of Men in theological Perspective*)

The continuing of Christ's apostolate

There is no good news unless this process of reconciliation is continued and is available to all subsequent generations—available but not repeated, extended but not added to or adapted. It is once and it is for all. Yet 'what He did for us must be done in us' (Anselm). So Jesus can say to his Apostles: 'As the Father has sent me even so send I you.' Jesus is able to extend in history by his will and therefore by his own choice, men essentially designated Apostles, in order that the essential character of their work and therefore the continuing Church shall be essentially apostolic. They are not qualified teachers necessarily nor are they necessarily exemplary in their Christian lives (though both are useful extras in the apostolic kit). Essentially they are the continuing of that one mission, which originates in the will of the Father, once and for all, to send forth his reconciling love in the person of Christ. Put in rather a different and perhaps rather a stark way, every absolution is the continuing of that once-for-all mission of the Father realised on the word of peace spoken in his Son. So in St Matthew 10:40, 'he who receives you receives me and he who receives me receives him who sent me.'

It is absurd to pretend that we can jump straight from the position of the apostolic ministry in the pages of the New Testament to the shape of ministry agreed by all scholars as prevalent by the middle of the second century. The Scriptures, the Creeds and the ministry of the Church are all the hazardous process of development and as such have the authority of the Holy Spirit at work in the Body of Christ by over-shadowing (ἐπισκεαζω) and so forming Christ and making him contemporary and present. It is so strange that some Christians can have a high doctrine of the formation of the Canon of Holy Scripture while having a 'low' doctrine of the ministry. The formation of the New Testament was not an immediate process and for a long time some books were included and some books were excluded. Nevertheless, slowly an agreed canon evolved which had the authority of Scripture as the word of God accepted by the people of God under the guidance of the Spirit of God. But this was not an immediate process and certainly took as long to evolve as the evolution of the apostolic ministry. The two resulting patterns of scripture and the ministry represent a development under the Holy Spirit. By the middle of the second century the apostolic ministry is still far from tidy but nevertheless it has some distinct characteristics and a definite shape; and the authority which the Church rightly attaches to that ministry is analogous to the authority of Holy Scripture since it is the evolution and development of the shape of the Church recognised with the authority of Christ's own apostolic ministry, accepted by the members of the Body of Christ, under the guidance of the Spirit of Christ.

The apostolic ministry of the Church essentially focussed then around the presence and person of the bishop through whom the high-priesthood functions in the life of the Church, and from whom all other apostolic ministry was derived. To many the doctrine of the episcopate in the Letters of St Ignatius of Antioch would seem excessive. What is certain is that he saw his own apostolic mission as rooted in and closely resembling the mission of Christ to the point of inevitably including the sacrificial death of martyrdom. Here is no mere cultic figure, claiming for the episcopate authority to perform rites and ceremonies, but rather Ignatius is essentially a moral figure closely allying the apostolic ministry in the person of the bishop with the same apostolic ministry of Christ. For both alike, sacrifice and martyrdom are inevitable by-products of a life lived in obedience to and derived from the mission of God the Father in sending His Son into the world. The authority of the bishop for Ignatius was not in any way a prelacy, it was not in any way rooted in a prelatical understanding of episcopacy but rather in the close identification between Jesus the Lord and the bishop as his representative both by his office and also in his personal life.

It is only later, long after the peace of Constantine, that the three-fold ministry comes to be regarded as a kind of *cursus honorum*, and the bishop begins to take to himself the identity of the prince and the king or the governor with all the secular overtones of prelacy. It is that figure which the Reformation rejected, but sadly felt unable to unpackage without abolishing. But the Church is not an organisation, it is an organism. For an organism any reformation or renewal cannot begin *de novo*. It is a longer process in which it is necessary to carry your history with you, and you do not attempt perfectionism or primitivism at each stage—going back to the beginning—for this is not possible in a living organism. All that you are, even after reformation, has been made possible by all that you have been before that act of reformation so that reformation and renewal in a living body will have about it a continuity as well as a discontinuity— 'things new' and 'things old'—in order that all things may be made new. 'There's no need for turning back, for all roads lead to where we stand' (Don Maclean *Crossroads*). The renewal of the episcopate is crucial in the renewal of the Church which takes its very identity from the apostolicity of the high-priestly ministry of Christ himself, focused in the bishop. In its very nature it is clothed in history and there is no going back behind that process in the hope of pulling out of the cupboard a long-forgotten model clothed only in the dust of antiquity. Primitivism is a dangerous disease which all too readily afflicts those who speak of renewal and reformation, and indeed it is also a dangerous disease which pervades much contemporary theology in its quest for a purer christology behind Chalcedon or a more authentic quest for the historic Jesus.

The bishop as the sign of unity

It is essential to emphasise the organic nature of the Church in the early days: organic rather than organisational. It had no structures or secretariat and all this at a time of rapid expansion and missionary extension. Although in the early days the Church was cradled within Judaism it soon broke loose into the pluralistic Greco-Roman world, and before very long it had grown far beyond the limits of the Mediterranean world. At each stage it had to be flexible and respond to the cultures and structures in which it found itself, yet it must be faithful by relating to, and being consistent with, the once-for-all apostolic mission of its founder. The miracle of the Church in the first centuries is its extraordinary unity within flexibility. Anyone with any sense of history, who has studied the changing patterns in institutions, could not help but be deeply struck by the organic flexibility of the Church and yet its surprising unity in the early centuries of its history.

In no small part, this was the result of the organic unity of the episcopate. It guaranteed a living link at every point of development—keeping the Church 'in touch with' itself. A bishop's authority did not depend upon his own gifts and qualifications but on his ability to trace the line of his authority to one of the great centres of apostolic life. This is already obvious, by contradiction even as early as New Testament times, in the somewhat tedious argument of St Paul in the opening chapters of his Epistle to the Galatians when he is tracing the source of his own authority and its relation to the Apostles.

This organic unity through the bishop enabled the Church to be diverse within unity; indigenous and yet universal. The once-for-all commission of Jesus: 'as the Father has sent me even so send I you' was extended, giving to the Church a consistency and continuity while permitting it to identify with, and involve itself in, the life of the culture in which it was located.

The role and person of the local presbyter was essentially related to the bishop: he was an extension of the episcopate and derived his authority and ministry from the bishop. Here indeed is an hierarchy but in its more fundamental sense—holy order. It is not necessary to see hierarchy in the shape of a pyramid but rather in the sense in which the Gospels are insistent that no one should be sent out alone, but rather two by two: so even today the bishop when he institutes a vicar speaks of 'this Cure which is both mine and thine'.

That ministry was essentially one of Word and sacraments: 'but we shall give ourselves to the ministry of the Word and prayer' (Acts 6:2–4). All kinds of other ministries are needed and administration is itself a ministry, but it is not the distinctive ministry of the bishop or of his local representative—the presbyter. The deacon is a ministry but a ministry from among the baptised; it is complementary to the episcopate and it is not necessarily a preparation for the priesthood. It stands in its own right not as a sign to the clergy of ministry but as a sign to the baptised of all their ministries and responsibilities. As the bishop is to the ordained ministry so is the deacon to the ministries of the laity. At the heart of the Church there is this sense of complementary ministry of which the bishop and the deacon are the outward and visible signs.

The ordained ministry is essentially there to order all the other ministries and to preserve holy order. When all the charismatic gifts of the ascended Christ are given to God's people, there will be many ministries from among the baptised—both men and women. The work of the episcopate and in its extension through the presbyterate will be essentially the work of overseeing—preserving 'the unity of the Spirit in the bond of peace' of which the Holy Communion is the outward and visible sign.

The sad truth is that it was not long before the ordained ministry in the history of the Church became a sort of one-man band—and at that the man was a conductor to boot! The charismatic ministries, for which Tertullian urged the people to pray on Easter Eve as the newly baptised emerged out of the waters of the font, were rapidly suppressed by the structural ministries of the ordained ministry. These charismatic ministries permeated the whole life of all the baptised in the early days so that Paul specifies a rather well-to-do and philanthropic lady named Phoebe as a 'deacon' of the Church at Corinth (Romans 16:1). There had for long been women deacons in the Christian Church who came forward and gave specialised ministry in caring for the poor and sick and of the baptism of other women. Women also shared in the highest gifts of the Spirit as we see in the case of Philip the Evangelist who had four daughters who were prophetesses (Acts 21:9), which is of course a continuation of the tradition of the Old Testament where both men and women shared in the ministry of prophecy. These, together with all the charismatic ministries, contributed a concept of ministry free from clericalism which was far more extensive than the apostolic ordained ministry of the bishop or of his local representative the priest.

The renewal of the Church today depends upon the renewal of a true episcopate, which in turn has the overseeing (not overbearing) of all those other ministries needing to relate to the whole Church in a single unity; for the charismatic needs the sacramental and in turn the sacramental needs the charismatic. Simon Tugwell writes in his book *Did you receive the Spirit?*:

> It is to be hoped that we shall see a general revival in the Church of all the various ministries and offices listed by St Paul. For too long the priest has had to shoulder the lot and he is most unlikely to be naturally or supernaturally equipped for it. He needs the prophets and healers, and those gifted with supernatural wisdom and knowledge. If all these charismatic ministries are revived, this will probably contribute more than anything else to the revival of the true charism of the priesthood, which will be freed from other burdens to be itself.

Episcopacy without prelacy
Beneath all the debris and rubble of ecclesiasticism, the figure of the

bishop has been crucial to any understanding of the Church as apostolic. He is the icon of Christ, the one priest of our Redemption. The word icon is important. It is a strong word in the Christian vocabulary, meaning the very opposite of a photograph: a photograph implies absence whereas an icon implies presence. The bishop in that sense is an image and icon of Christ. He holds this position not because he is a qualified saint but because he is a chosen sinner. In his office he is a Gospel figure; hopefully and by grace and humility he might also reflect something of this in his person, but the survival of the episcopate in history has relied upon his choice and election as a sinner thankfully rather than upon his qualifications as a saint. The signs of his office—hopefully not totally contradicted in his person—are Gospel signs and are part of that icon.

The mitre is not a crown, it is a sacramental sign of his anointing in the Spirit. It is essentially a reminder of the tongues of fire, and whatever outward decoration it may bear, its inner colour should be the red of fire, and its shape should be pointed and not rounded like a tea-cosy. The lappets, which are a continuing inconvenience to the wearer, are not just decoration. In the very early ceremonies of the consecration of a bishop, the open Scriptures were laid, as a yoke across the back of the shoulders of the new apostolic figure. He was to be a man under the authority of the revelation of the Scriptures. He might have all kinds of interesting opinions on all kinds of subjects, but his office as a bishop was essentially grounded in his obedience to the authority of Scripture and to the revelation which it contains. The two lappets were reduced rapidly into two book-markers for the Old and New Testaments. What an uncomfortable and inconvenient reminder they can be: they often get in the way! The answer is not just to cut them off (as I saw one Anglican bishop had done recently) but rather to let them rest on the shoulders where they belong and where they most suitably are intended to be. For the measure of the authority of the Church will be the measure of its obedience to the revelation of Christ. Obedience and authority belong together: Christ spoke with authority about the Father and the things of the Father because he had first learnt the obedience of a Son.

So with the ring—it is not simply a piece of ecclesiastical jewellery. It is a sign of the Gospel. Since the early centuries the bishop's stone has been the amethyst, which by derivation from the Greek means, 'not to be drunk'. The first bishop began his first sermon: 'We are not drunk, we are filled with the Holy Spirit.' It is a refreshing thought to imagine the break-up of the Lambeth Conference leading newspaper reporters and passers-by to conclude that the conference had in effect been a drinking party! It would be a happy correction if a Press statement had to be issued by the Archbishop of Canterbury: 'We are not drunk, we are filled with the Holy Spirit!' In the meantime it might be important for the bishop to continue to wear a ring evoking the possibility of that confusion between drunkenness and Pentecost which was so evident at the beginning of the mission of the Church.

The crook needs little explanation, except to say that it is not a staff or a mace but a humble shepherd's crook—a sign of risk and of recovery, of prompting and of cautioning—the *pastor pastorum* who is ready to lay down his life for the sheep. We need to recover these symbols not for reasons of sentimentality, but to rescue this office of the bishop from a false prelacy from the past and equally from the false models of management and job-description which plague the present secularisation of the Church. The bishop does not have a throne, but a humble teaching-chair, and the cathedral is the familiar household of faith—the mother church of the diocese where the faithful can feel most at home.

In all these ways, the bishop is intended to be an icon of the Gospel, and his person and presence should declare the nature of his mission and the source of his authority. It was Austin Farrer who was not ashamed to apply to the person of a bishop, the phrase, 'a walking sacrament'. In all this, the key to his person and his authority in the Church, is nothing less than Christ himself in his priesthood, in which service and authority belong together: among God's people 'as one who serves'.

Priesthood not clericalism

The stability of the episcopate should find its flexible extension in the gregarious nature of the priesthood. For the priesthood is essentially the same in character as the episcopate, and shares the essential elements of the apostolicity of the episcopal office. It is the local extension of the ordained ministry, with the essential characteristics of oversight for the sake of unity, that encourages the local indigenous and charismatic ministries and yet expresses the sacramental unity of the local church both within itself and in its universal relationship to the wider Church.

The priest, therefore, is not just the 'natural' president. It is dangerous to ask the reductionist question: 'What can a priest do that a baptised Christian cannot do?' and then come up with the reply: 'Preside at the Eucharist and absolve.' These two functions are an inevitable and outward sign of the priest's inner relationship (by office rather than by function) to the local Christian body on the one hand and the wider Church on the other. Both of them are sacraments and signs of unity and reconciliation, and in these two signs he relates as much to the bishop as to the local congregation and is as much a representative of God as he is a representative of the people. Much recent discussion and writing about the idea of the priest again misses this double expression of his nature and begins to talk dangerously about self-authentication and local and indigenous ministries.

The one thing that an apostolic-ordained ministry cannot be is simply indigenous. Again and again as I have gone around the parishes in the diocese (and not least the country parishes where indigenous ministry is so often defended), the local priest has talked of cliques and divisions, social and otherwise, in the parish. He alone as the man sent from the outside to the situation is the one figure who can be truly representative and not divisive in any local situation. In any case we have our Lord's own words on this very matter: 'A prophet is not without honour save in his own country.' An indigenous ministry might well focus a kind of comfortable local 'ecclesiastical freemasonry', but it would lack that very thrust of prophetic apostolic ministry which alone can create a local gathering both local and universal, resembling the natural groups of the parish and yet in another sense equally quite unlike any other group on earth. The local church will only be truly catholic if it is also apostolic.

Nevertheless we need to experiment with a priesthood which is not bound up in clericalism on the one hand and, because it relates to the bishop and the rest of the diocese, is not merely congregationalist on the other hand, running its own show in a mini-cathedral and creating only the 'church thing'. The local priest needs to have the charism to discern all the other charisms and to be a natural trainer to build up the whole body, free from a wrong dependence, in which the baptised take a full part in the church and in the extensive ministries outlined in the New Testament.

The ministry of the baptised

Such a Church will release and empower ministry in all baptised men and women. That ministry will be released and centred within the life of the body and will also spill over into the life of the wider community. 'By this shall men know that you are my disciples, that you love one another.' Put like that it could make the Church sound most frightfully ingrown, and yet unless there is the warmth and solidarity of the fellowship of the Spirit at the heart of the Christian life, we can lose the essential complementarity of the second commandment: 'Love your neighbour *as* yourself.' The community of the baptised is essentially the forgiven, forgiving community and experiences within itself the totality of the Gospel. It is from this community, in which love and forgiveness and ministry are given and received, that the apostolic ministry is charged for its work in the world. 'They then sent out Paul and Barnabas' (Acts 13:3). Here again apostolic commission reflects the initiative of the apostolic mission of Christ sent by the Father in the power of the Spirit out of the environment of the Trinity where love is given and received. ('Father let us have together the love we had before the world began') The Church is not a gathering of enterprising individuals trying to help the world and to do good. It is the reservoir from which the rivers of love overflow (to use the analogy of St Bernard). Today, as in his day, there are still too many rivers and not enough reservoirs!

Each man, woman and child is baptised for ministry. Lacordaire writes: 'The Christian is the man to whom Christ confides others.' 'No passengers aboard this ship: crew only.' Those words might well be the slogan over the entrance to Christ's ark, because for too long the ordained ministry has run the show rather like a luxury liner with deck service, latterly deteriorating (with the shortage of clergy)

to a help-yourself cafeteria. However the day must surely dawn
when we realise that there are no passengers aboard this ship—only
crew. The ordained ministry has suppressed the other ministries and
yet the ascended gifts of Christ in Ephesians are for the equipping of
the saints for the work of the total ministry, and it is these very gifts
and charisms for which the Church should pray in both the vigil of
Ascensiontide as well as at the font on Easter Eve. It is not true to say
that women have been kept out of the ministry: rather men and
women alike have been kept out of ministry by the tyranny of the
ordained ministry in all the tradition of the Churches. The Reformation did nothing to put this right. It is for the restoration of this fuller
concept of ministry that we should struggle and work and pray, for
only so will we release the ordained priesthood from clericalism to be
the subtle ministry of loving-oversight, preserving 'the unity of the
Spirit in the bond of peace'.

But the ministry of the baptised must be careful that it does not
become more clericalised than the clergy! The phrase 'the priesthood
of all believers' is not the same as the priesthood of every believer.

> The priesthood of the ministry follows as a corollary from the
> priesthood of the Church. What the one is, the other is ... The
> ordained priests are priestly because it is the Church's prerogative
> to be priestly; and because they are, by ordination; specialized and
> empowered to exercise ministerially and organically the preroga-
> tives of the body as a whole ... We utterly protest against the
> unauthorised *sequitur* which would conclude that therefore the
> powers of the whole can be exercised by any or all. It is not given
> to the eye to hear, nor the ear to see. Those who actually celebrate
> do but organically represent, and act for the whole. (R. C. Mob-
> erly *Ministerial Priesthood*)

The whole church is a priestly body and in its relationship to God and
the world exercises the total priesthood of Christ by being his Body
and by enacting that once-for-all act of reconciliation which focuses
most clearly upon the Passion, Death and Resurrection of Christ.
The ordained priest is there for the sake of the Church: the Church is
there for the sake of the world. I am not sure that lay readers are not

often rather more regarded as liturgical ministers than as a sign to all the baptised community of their responsibility for ministry through baptism. It is perhaps hardly surprising that lay readers focus more in the liturgy because that is largely the basis of the charge which is given to them. This focus, however, should be seen as the exception in lay ministry rather than the norm. We need men and women as healers and prophets, teachers and hospital visitors; to distribute the sacraments and to care for the poor, and the lonely and the bereaved. There is especially a ministry of prayer and intercession for widows, who should always have a special place in the life of the Church. In short, never before has the Church so much needed an icon of what it is to be a true layman. (To many people Sir Thomas More has been just one such example of history.) Furthermore much lay ministry should focus around the house, the small group or place of work and should not necessarily focus on the church building at all. It is the life of the Church from Monday to Saturday which determines the authenticity of its worship on the Lord's day and the great days.

Only in this way will the Church be renewed for ministry under the oversight of the bishop and his representative—the parish priest.

Practical reflections and applications

1 *Pastoral strategy for the Church*   At the present time the Church in Western society is standing at the crossroads in its relationship to society at large and in a sense it gets the worst of both options. Should it still seek to speak for society at large, ministering to its religious needs on great occasions, burying the dead, baptising, and relating to all the other structures of society at a structural and institutional level? Or, on the other hand, should the Christian Churches accept that numerically they are a small percentage of the total population in a religiously pluralistic society, and seek to work more and more as an underground minority group, ministering mainly if not solely to the committed, and observing a fairly fixed line between the Church and the rest of society?

Certainly in England, if we take the strategy of the Roman Catholic Communion as an interesting model over the past century, it bears careful study. Here was a Church which in 1830 had no hierarchy, no cathedrals, no bishops and was a minority Church, less in number and strength than Nonconformity and not even regarded as a serious part of the religious spectrum in 19th-century England. It promoted its work largely by ministering only to its own, propagating its faith through its schools while being largely unrepresented in the media. It had a strong profile and a clear identity. Nevertheless in just over one hundred years this method of pastoral strategy has resulted in the Roman Communion being the second largest Church in the British Isles only just short of the Anglican Church and way ahead of the churches of Nonconformity. Far from resulting in an ingrown Church it holds as much effective presence and power as the Church of England yet it stands free from establishment and (certainly to the outsider) appears as flexible and as well equipped for missionary work in this country as any other Christian body.

We might therefore be tempted to suppose that we should pursue the missionary strategy of the Church today, in a largely non-Christian culture, in the way in which Roman Catholics have pursued their mission over the past hundred years. On the other hand it must be said that the present climate in Western Europe has not positively rejected Christianity and still chooses to associate itself largely with the Christians and with the Church-thing to a very large extent. Of course it would be neater at the edges if there were clearer and more definite lines between those who go to church and those who do not. Although that is much more so as each year passes, it is not completely the case and any good and sensitive pastor will still seize every opportunity from a carol service to a harvest festival, a watchnight service to a wedding, to encourage and relate to this largely inarticulate faith which still persists and pervades just beneath the surface of our national life.

Surely it is possible to do this and yet at the same time for the Church to shed much of the ecclesiasticism and to become communities living in the fellowship of the Spirit and in the power of the Death and Resurrection of Jesus. While maintaining a clear curriculum of public services it must be possible to extend these and to be much more flexible with not only the Sunday timetable but also with a stronger collective life during the week. For the true picture today is evident in that the mainsprings of the life of the Church no longer pass through the culture of our age. Suenens writes:

> At a time when the ship is being battered we ought to offer to God
> and his Church a fidelity that is even more pure and stable. Our
> fidelity ought to be purer because it relies no longer on the
> sociological underpinnings of a Christian culture that is disappear-
> ing, but upon God himself, who is experienced in our more
> personal concern and apostolic commitment. Our fidelity is more
> stable because we must go through and beyond the weaknesses of
> the Church and know how to recognise and love its true face.

'We can no longer rely on the sociological pinnings of a Christian
culture that is disappearing.' There is the point. We must minister to
the culture and give and receive from it, but we cannot rely upon it as
giving to the Church the strategy for its pastoral care and its missionary opportunities. In that sense I do not believe that the world can
write the agenda for the Church.

Schools are ceasing to teach (in spite of the Education Act of 1944)
anything remotely approaching the Christian faith. Our educational
programme for the Church must extend and include all people at all
stages of their development. The Durham Report long ago pointed
out that any specifically Christian education in any of the mainstream traditions of the Church would increasingly be the sole
responsibility of the Churches. Each diocese and deanery must have
its own training programme and increasingly put larger and larger
quantities of its eggs into its training basket for both clergy and laity
alike.

2 *The place of the bishop in the Church today*   Stripped of prelacy,
the bishop must still be the focus of renewal in the Church. He is not
another order above and beyond the order of priesthood: he is
priesthood in its fullest and richest expression. When I first became a
bishop after a lively ministry among students in London University,
and after the deep and enriching pastorate of All Saints', Margaret
Street, and the Institute of Christian Studies, I could not understand
what had happened to me or to my ministry. It was as though I was
in a totally different dimension. All those things which had fed and

enriched my ministry—consecutive and consistent preaching, teaching and visiting, hearing of confessions and spiritual direction—were taken from me. As I put my key in the front door of my house at the end of the day, I realised that I lived my days now in a life largely outside the environment of the Church whose chief pastor I was supposed to be. Of course there are all kinds of ways of manipulating this state of affairs and my fellow bishops were patient and kind in showing me the ropes. Nevertheless, it was a shock to find that episcopacy was not necessarily the flowering of one's priesthood but rather a different job with a new job-description.

I am certain that this is wrong. The bishop must be part of the environment of the Church, not just confirming the catechumenate, but being himself part and at the very heart of the work of preparing that catechumenate and in an environment in which he is available both to clergy and laity alike. In this process he will give and he will receive. Ideally, of course, such an environment is the cathedral. In this way, bishops need to learn to live once again in the context of the liturgical and training life of the Church, readily accessible to their clergy and in the main stream of mission.

Should we have more bishops? This is a difficult question to answer. In many ways it would seem logical to make most borough deans into bishops, but I am not certain this is the best way forward. I am not certain that to increase the top of the mushroom would not result in the Church's being more clerical than it is at the present time. The real break-through will come only by increasing the expectation of what it is just to be a Christian—to strengthen the roots of the Church, and not to increase its branches. The club-mentality of running 'a show' in the local parishes with various clubs within the club, is not the shape of a pastorate, or of a parish. It is true that such a pastorate is a full-time and demanding task to all of the clergy that we have at the present time. We need to re-orientate the life and expectation of the whole Body of Christ in all the parishes in which the priest has his distinctive part to play before we can decide whether or not we need more priests or even more bishops. Each parish must see itself essentially as a training unit until it becomes increasingly centred on ministry in the fullest sense of the word, serviced by the apostolic representative—the parish priest. The priest in his turn must relate closely to his bishop as a source of all apostolic endeavour.

3 *A diversity of spirituality*   We speak today so often about a shortage of priests. What we should be speaking about more is a right use of priests. It is true that all the Churches of the Reformation have become increasingly eucharistically-centred in recent years and this is a healthy and a good sign. However, although the Eucharist is the characteristic expression of Christian life, it is not the exclusive expression of Christian life. In the 18th century, the Methodist revival was grounded in the creation of a spirituality which was Bible-centred with its prayer groups and study groups. It was this diversity of spirituality which was one of the greatest contributions which the Methodist Church had to make in any reunion of the Churches. For here was a spirituality not wholly dependent upon clergymen or priest-centred.

The Roman Catholic Communion today is creating a diversity of spiritualities which, although they focus on the Mass, are not wholly and exclusively dependent upon the Mass. The Little Brothers of Charles de Foucauld with their strong lay associates, and the Focalare groups are but two such spiritualities. We need through all the Churches to meet frequently as Christians for prayer and Bible study, for the reading of the psalms and for singing of spiritual songs, for the Office and for intercession and adoration before the Blessed Sacrament. These should just be some of the characteristics of the day-to-day spirituality of the Church which would not be wholly dependent upon the local priest. Never perhaps since the earliest days (if even then) have Christians made their communion more frequently and (sadly) more casually. This is not a good sign. We need other corporate expressions of our Christian life and growth. Above all we want a growth in depth and in quality of Christian life, lived by the *plebs sancta dei* from Monday to Saturday, rooted in the everyday life of society. We shall not get this only and simply by multiplying the number of priests or by stepping up the number of times that the Eucharist is celebrated and the faithful receive their communion.

5. BUT WHY ON EARTH THE CHURCH AT ALL?

Jesus, but not the Church

It is fascinating to see how the person of Jesus Christ is still so alive and so vivid to our civilisation—not least among young people and at the popular level. Not only is there a return to an interest in religion in general, but in particular to the person of Jesus as a great religious figure, the man for others, and the man of simplicity and poverty. *Jesus Christ Superstar* and *Godspell* succeeded in taking the scriptural accounts of the New Testament about the life and teaching of Jesus and producing them as box-office successes without distorting the figure of Jesus to the point of offence, and in many ways presenting him with a freshness and authenticity which many thousands of clergy and devout Christian people found challenging and helpful. In the realm of the new secular mysticism of the seventies, the person of Jesus took his place and seemed to speak to a wide cross-section of people—people who largely never darkened the doors of the churches.

Jesus, yes—but, the Church, no! When I go round schools and universities and field a free-for-all question-and-answer session, of the four clauses of the Creed—belief in God, belief in Jesus, belief in the Holy Spirit, belief in the Church—the first three seem accepted and believed by most people in some sense, but it is the Church which is largely under attack and not to be found anywhere on the agenda. Put rather crudely—Jesus is in, but the Church is out.

Ecclesiasticism

Some of the current rejection of the Church is part of the wider rejection of institutions in general and of the Establishment in particular, and perhaps should be taken neither more nor less seriously than any other vogue. Nevertheless behind the smoke-screen of much second-hand criticism there is a wealth of genuine protest which we would do well to heed.

There is lurking in the collective subconsciousness of 'the man in the street' an image of the Church which is largely fed by the images of medieval bishops and saints and of holy men and of holy women, of prayer, simplicity of life, poverty and openness to the Spirit, and while it is wrong for the Church (or for anyone) simply to fulfil popular images and expectations, there must at least be some *over-lapping* between the image and subconscious symbol and its contemporary representation. The revival of Christianity will not start six feet above popular images and symbols and totally unrelated to them. The institutional Church with its image of relevance, and the religionless Christianity of the sixties, was an interesting intellectual purging, but it had about it that total discontinuity which fails to connect with anything at the more profound level of the collective subconscious in what remains of the English-speaking religious sensitivity. I suppose I am into a very dangerous area here—the area of folk religion—and yet I believe that a truly catholic appeal and a catholic evangelism can never really totally disregard what for want of a better phrase I would call this element of folk religion. Neither in one sense should it. For if the Incarnation is 'to take'—as it were—it has no other place to start than in the murky roots of folk religion, and there is more of that in most of us than most of us might care to admit. There is no such thing as pure spirit—or if there is it is something rather like lightning that humankind cannot handle. The only thing to do with lightning is to earth it and so with the Holy Spirit. In doing so it 'picks up' much of folk religion but hopefully redirects it, for religion, like everything else, needs redeeming. It needs redeeming but not emasculating or merely intellectualising, and there are many who think that providing something is 'on the brain' that it is then all right. But religion, rather like sex, is safer when it is earthed and certainly the worst place to have it is on the brain!

So little wonder that, if some were striving in the sixties for a religionless Church, there will be others who in the seventies will strive for a churchless religion. When the Beatles became curious about spiritual kicks it was not to the monasteries or the clergy that they turned but rather to the Eastern mystics of India. Or, more crudely in the book and film *The Exorcist*, the priest with the effective power against evil was, when the chips were down, not the intellectual reductionist, with-it clergyman, free from the superstitions of the past, but the old-fashioned priest who looked 'spiritual' and even holy and who not only believed in the Devil but could name him and cast him out. It is not incidental that the name which Eskimo Indians give to the bishop means, literally, the 'chief praying man'.

In other words the contemporary world will not dismiss the priest or religious figure because he is holier-than-thou, but rather because he is not holy enough. And again if this is put more crudely perhaps bishops must look a little more like Jesus, for every bishop (and many priests) has had his cassock pulled by a little child with the shattering question, 'Are you Jesus?'

Put in another way, the Church must be an effective symbol of the body of Christ and a symbol which overlaps with, and connects with, the subconscious if it is to be effective. Part of the task of renewal involves the uncovering of the features of the Body of Christ on earth. Or put in the words of Cardinal Suenens, 'We must go through and beyond the weaknesses of the Church and know how to recognise and love its true face.' We cannot dispense with institutions or structures: for part of being an historical and incarnate body is that we are clothed with history and with institutions, but the structure and the institutions must be the servants and not the masters of the end to which they should point.

Neither can we become simply a spiritual Church—the Incarnation demands that the feet of the Body of Christ are rooted in clay—the clay of history and politics, and heavy with the past. For there is no ascension which can be good news for the world until there has been a baptism and descending into the earth. The point of

Christian renewal is not so much that it should rise to heaven but that it should first collect up all of the earth in order that in its ascension the fragments are gathered up and nothing remains left behind as merely of the earth. A spiritual Church is literally no earthly use. But on the other hand, the Church must continually uncover and rediscover the effective icon which is nothing less than the features of Christ himself and as such will have a universal appeal and attractiveness, for there is such a reality as 'the beauty of holiness'.

> The mistake of ecclesiasticism through the ages has been to believe in the Church as a kind of thing-in-itself. The Apostles never regarded the Church as a thing-in-itself. Their faith was in God who had raised Jesus from the dead, and they knew the power of his Resurrection to be at work in them and in their fellow-believers despite the unworthiness of them all. . . . That is always the nature of true belief in the Church. It is a laying hold of the power of the Resurrection. (Michael Ramsay: *The Future of the Church*)

Such a challenge to every priest and bishop and every congregation is to rescue the Church from being just a thing-in-itself, and rather to see that it glorifies the one whose apostolic charge it first received and in him and through him to glorify the Father. The Church must not point men to itself but beyond itself, in the same way as Jesus did not glorify himself but glorified the one who sent him. In a word the Church must not point to itself but to the kingdom.

The Church and the Kingdom

All three analogies in the New Testament for the Christian individually or corporately are analogies which point away from themselves: salt, light, leaven. The salt is not a meal in itself or an end in itself; good lighting illuminates its surroundings and does not draw attention to itself; leaven is lost in the lump. So the Church is not the kingdom but rather it points men to the kingdom, as Jesus points men to the Father. The evangelistic call of the Church is not so much, 'Come and join us,' as 'Look: listen: wake up.' 'God is active in his

world, in the nation and in your life. This day is set before you the
way of life and of death: choose life.' The Church is not the kingdom
although it overlaps with the kingdom sometimes more and sometimes less; and certainly, when in history it has tried to be the
kingdom or associated itself with the kingdom as though it were
co-terminous with that kingdom, it has been at its most corrupt. At
its best the Church has not held the centre of the stage but rather held
a different relation both to the world on the one hand and to the
kingdom on the other.

This has largely been the prophetic element within the Church and
has enabled the Church both to join with all men of goodwill in the
pursuit of the ends and aims of the kingdom (whatever their creed,
their credentials or motives) but at the same time to sit lightly to the
world in a true poverty of spirit, 'having nothing yet possessing all
things, as unknown yet well known'. In so many ways the Churches
are conscious today of a break-down in their institutional life; numerically all of them have shrunk, and yet if this break-down will
enable a new break-through of the Holy Spirit through a true poverty of spirit, such a chapter in history as our own could well be
more conspicuous for renewal and for true growth than almost any
previous chapter in our history. 'The Church of England as it now
stands no human power can save,' wrote Arnold in 1832. Yet 1832 is
not conspicuous as the year of break-down in the life of the Church
but rather as the year of break-through and new beginnings in the
shape of the Oxford Movement, the Evangelistic Revival and the
largest missionary expansion since the beginning of Christian history. Perhaps this was possible only because both Evangelicals and
Oxford churchmen alike realised that the salvation of the Church of
England did not depend upon 'human power'. For too long the
Churches had rested upon human power and relied upon their
'secular underpinnings', and so had failed to relate either to the
kingdom in a true and prophetic way or to the world in a loving and
corrective way.

It could be that our present seeming ineffectiveness is part of that
unpacking of past relationships which have grown false with age,
and if these relationships could be re-ordered in true humility and
poverty of spirit it could open the flood-gates to a true renewal of the

Holy Spirit. For the work of the Holy Spirit is to form Jesus, as at the Annunciation, and we are best filled with Holy Spirit, as the Magnificat itself proclaims, when we are empty, hungry and expectant. 'He hath put down the mighty from their seat and hath exalted the humble and meek: he hath filled the hungry with good things and the rich he hath sent empty away.' No man can receive anything when he is full of self-importance or self-pity. The Church today needs rescuing from both alike, if it is to be truly open to renewal and to being filled afresh with Holy Spirit. For always the work of the Spirit is to form and reform the Body of Jesus.

Spirit of the living God fall afresh on me.

Such is the prelude to all true renewal.

It is as though there were three Bodies of Christ: the Body of Christ physical in the person of Jesus Christ in first-century Palestine; the Body of Christ, sacramental on the altar; and the Body mystical in the life of the members of the Church in any age and in any part of the world in all ages and everywhere. These three 'testimonies' must agree if the Church is to have an authentic ring and to demand our allegiance. It is as though these three realities were one, and yet they have become shattered and set over and against each other. On the one hand, there are those who want to talk only about Jesus of Nazareth in isolation. On the other, there are those who are concerned only with the cult of the Mass and the concept of the body of Christ, sacramental. Then there are those who are passionately concerned to make the membership of the Christian Church a living and credible reality. All three of these facets of the Body of Christ should endorse one another, for each is the work of the 'overshadowing' of the Holy Spirit, so that in that sense we must indeed pray for a charismatic release and charismatic renewal in order that the Church on earth may effectively be known and recognised as what it is—the Body of Christ. Cardinal Suenens writes:

> We Christians, used to accepting indiscriminately as one whole the pure gold of the Gospel and the wrappings of human making, have got to be trained to discern the difference. It is not easy to

restore the interior of a Gothic cathedral covered with baroque or modern plaster and to recover its original lines. To restore a cathedral like some Viollet le Duc requires more than momentary enthusiasm.

It will require nothing less than the 'overshadowing' of that Holy Spirit to come upon us and the power of the Holy Spirit to dwell within us in order that that which is formed in us may be holy—the Body of Christ.

The three Bodies of Christ
'You are the Body of Christ, that is to say, in you and through you the method of the work of the Incarnation must go on. You are meant to incarnate in your own lives the theme of your adoration. You are to be taken, consecrated, broken and distributed, that you may be the means of grace and vehicles of the Eternal Charity' (St Augustine). Jesus took the bread, gave thanks for it and blessed it, and gave it and said, 'This is me: this is my life—this is your life: this is what life is all about.' Allowing for the parodying to some extent of the words of Institution it is not too much to say the distinctive and characteristic attitude of Jesus to life was eucharistic and that the words and actions of the institution of the Eucharist are intended to be the words and actions which characterise the Body of Christ in all three of its facets—physical, sacramental and mystical. Jesus handled life the same way as he handled that bread. Certainly in his post-Resurrection appearance on the road to Emmaus, the minute he sat down and took bread and broke it, they knew him. They would have recognised that anywhere! The identity of Jesus and his destiny are inextricably bound up with that piece of bread.

If so, there are really only three important miracles in the world. Each of them requires faith to discern it and not merely sight, and each of them is the work of the Holy Spirit. The first of the three questions might be phrased in this way: 'How on earth could God *take* human form, bless it, be broken in it, and die and rise again and give himself for the life of the world?' That is the Corpus Christi of Palestine two thousand years ago. Then there is the second miracle:

'How on earth can a piece of bread be taken, blessed, broken and given and be called in any real sense the Body of Christ—the Corpus Christi of matter?' That is the miracle of the altar. Then—and this is perhaps the greatest miracle of all: 'How on earth can ordinary men and women, thrown together with all kinds of motives, from all kinds of different backgrounds and starting points, be in any real sense called the Body of Christ when the priest turns to the congregation with the arrogant assertion "we are the Body of Christ"—the Corpus Christi in the face of humankind?'

For a long time the Church in its eucharistic discussions isolated the Corpus Christi of the altar and was obsessed almost exclusively with the Body of Christ sacramental, but there are in effect three 'witnesses' and all these three 'must agree' (1 John 5). For the truth is that the physical, sacramental and mystical must each share the same identity and the same destiny. Is it too much to see these three aspects played out in the history of Christian theology itself? For roughly the first eight hundred years after Christ, discussion about the person of Jesus was to be in the forefront of theology. It is the continuing repetition of the question addressed to Peter at Caesarea Philippi: 'Who do men say that I am?' 'Whose son is he?' Here is the christological discussion focusing around the Corpus Christi of Jesus, physical, and how he is to be seen and discerned in history in Palestine. Then during the next eight hundred years there are the battles about Jesus and his presence in the Eucharist: 'What happens to that piece of bread?' Or to repeat the little word of the Old Testament—'manna'—meaning 'What is it?' Here the emphasis is on the Corpus Christi of the Eucharist, the Body sacramental. But the preoccupation of theology since the 17th century has been with the nature of the Church itself, the identity of the Christian, who he is and what he is—the Corpus Christi of the Church militant, the Corpus Christi mystical. No doubt the pattern is a convenient retrospective 'myth', superimposed on a historical development which is far more untidy in reality; but nevertheless what is important is that these three testimonies must agree.

The miracle is the same throughout. 'How can these things be?' asks the Virgin Mary at the Annunciation. The answer to the Blessed Virgin is the same answer in the case of all three of these mysteries,

'By the overshadowing of the Holy Spirit.' The 'overshadowing' of the Holy Spirit is important in all three miracles if we are to understand them rightly—the overshadowing of the Holy Spirit at the conception of the Body of Christ; the Epiclesis on the altar in order that Christ may be formed and made present in our midst sacramentally and the overshadowing of the Holy Spirit (charismatic release) for the formation of the Body of Christ mystical among the people of God.

Discerning the Body of Christ

How can we discern the Body? Certainly appearances are not much help, and certainly if we limit our discernment to the sense of sight only, we shall be betrayed. Jesus in Palestine was in some sense as much a stumbling-block to the discernment of his identity as the bread—only too apparently bread upon the altar—and as the foibles and failings writ large upon the face of the congregation only all too obviously sinful, weak and mortal. All three of these affirmations about the Body of Christ are affirmations of a mystery of our faith. 'Outward sight' does not really aid or 'befriend' our 'senses'. So Christ replies to the inquiry of John the Baptist from prison with the words to his disciples: 'Go back and tell John ... blessed is he who does not find in me a stumbling-block.' Yes, happy indeed those who did not see his 'face' in Palestine. Happy indeed those who have *not* seen and have believed. For there is one element of prophesy that would say that the face of Christ had 'no beauty that we should desire him' in the flesh. The stumbling-block to faith is the obvious, the immediate and the material world impinging upon our senses: bypass the material in the name of the spiritual if you like, for that is always an easier route, but it is not the route of faith. The route of faith overtakes the test of sight and embraces the apparent contradiction which is presented to our senses.

So then how do we discern the Body of Jesus whether in Palestine, Jesus in the Sacrament of the altar, or Jesus in the life of his people? We discern it in actions, of course, which speak louder than words. But Christian spirituality and Christian morality have relied so very heavily upon words, dogmas and formulae. Where are the people in whom the action of taking, blessing, breaking and giving are really being played out? Where are God's eucharistic people? Where are the people whose destiny is strangely interwoven with this divine pattern—this shape of things to come? If Dom Gregory Dix could speak of 'The Shape of the Liturgy', do we not need to extend that concept of 'shape' into every aspect of Christian spirituality so that all the 'witnesses agree'? It would mean, of course, taking the four-fold pattern of the Eucharist and expanding it in just the way that St Augustine suggests in the above quotation. The quality of life which can become spiritual life (Resurrection life) must have the same fourfold shape as that bread which becomes our 'bread of life' or the drink which becomes our 'spiritual drink'.

This is our life
Let us therefore look at the fourfold action itself, for this may give us a clue to the identity of the Church on earth and the shape and pattern of the life of God's people. The taking of the bread is of the same order as the taking of the flesh of the Virgin Mary—an uncondi-tional, totally uncompromising acceptance of life as it is. Here is no romanticism or spiritualism, but rather a head-on collision and embracing between the things of heaven and the things of earth, the things of the Spirit and the things of the flesh. This is the very essence of what the Incarnation is all about, for 'what he did not *take* he did not redeem' (Anselm). This is no fantasy. It is the terrifying and awesome reality of what we mean by the Incarnation and it is still the fundamental doctrine of the Church. The blessing through taking is a total re-ordering of life so that all life may be seen to be as a gift. The hands which took the bread never took it for granted, but received it back again as a gift and in so doing bestowed a blessing. But the destiny of man cannot be fulfilled this side of such a total re-ordering and reforming which nothing less than a break with the old way of seeing things can achieve. For we have always seen things back to front and the wrong way round. The re-ordering and the essential change at the very heart of Christian life assumes the reality of 'death'. Perhaps we best understand that death by a quality of life which takes us to the point where we are out of our depth. Baptism is

the sign of this death. Essentially baptism is a sign of drowning and is a sign of the whole quality of the risen life which can begin only the *other side* of that point when we are out of our depth—when we are finished—and he can begin. It marks the Red Sea and although there is a continuity between the old and the new and between nature and Grace, between flesh and blood and the Kingdom of heaven, nevertheless there is also a discontinuity which is symbolised in the crossing of that Red Sea and in the drowning of our baptism as well as in the breaking of the bread in the Eucharist. This re-ordering, and the essential change of heart which it portrays, is at the very centre of Christian life and assumes the reality of death. In its turn that death comes to be seen paradoxically as the new and living way of life. Here is the divine contradiction which is at the very heart of the identity of God's people. Brother Roger Schutz, the Prior of Taizé, says that the Christian is himself a sign of contradiction. The words of Jesus: 'He who would keep his life will lose it, but he who will lose his life for my sake shall keep it to eternal life' (St John 12:25).

So the same hand which took the bread raised that hand in blessing, and it is the same hand that was nailed to a Cross. He died that we might live. In a real sense he died to live. But then, of course, the point of it all is the distribution to all men of the 'Eternal Charity'— the distribution not to 'the five thousand' only but to that great multitude which no man can number. The shape of the liturgy is indeed the shape of things to come. It is a whole attitude to life, and the Christian life is a mystery of faith signifying unto us 'the mystical union which is betwixt Christ and his Church'. But if our theology is not to be simply substitutionary, then what he did *for* us must be done *in* us, and so the eucharistic shape will be seen as flooding into every aspect of Christian life, into Christian theology, into the mission of the Church and the ecumenical quest. For they will all be seen, discerned and authenticated not merely in pragmatic and immediately visible terms, but rather as part of the proclaimation of the mystery of faith itself. This is especially true in the realm of spirituality and moral theology. Put in another way things are not what they seem to be, and outward appearances are never enough in discerning the divine activity.

We can work this out in terms of moral theology. Hence we must not covet. We must not covet because what is life is not *our* life but life as a gift. The Eucharist formula is a mandate for a whole new outlook upon life and a revolution, spreading to all things new as well as old. For man needs a whole new attitude to life, a new attitude to others, to the environment, to wages and just rewards, to matters of illness and misfortune which only a eucharistic attitude and pattern can sufficiently illuminate and direct.

For the 'taking' is itself a witness to the sort of love which is the love of God and which is eternal. Therefore the sacrament of matrimony is the first and obvious spilling over of the eucharistic pattern, that takes us to the very heart and meaning of vows in every vocation. 'For better, for worse; for richer, for poorer; in sickness and in health, till death us do part . . . ' Such words can neither be vindicated in pragmatic terms of compatibility, nor in moralistic terms about the place of divorce and separation. They point rather to a quality of acceptance, a first step in the right direction without which we can never grow up. Yet this cannot be contested for solely under the heading of 'moral theology' or under any theological heading of a departmentalised kind. Essentially it witnesses to something which we can discern now only by faith and not by sight—though love bears witness also in a loving heart. Christ is in effect saying to us: 'You will never find out what life is really all about till you learn to take it in the same way as I took you and as I take the bread—unconditionally and uncompromisingly. Now let's take marriage for example . . . ' But of course, such a quality of loving acceptance both requires maturity and brings maturity, yet before all else it requires faith matched by grace. For it is a sharing and communion in the very quality of love which binds God to man, and binds the blessed Persons of the Trinity to one another in unity. Christian marriage is a witnessing of the inner quality of all love and all life. It is in such an outlook that there is no need to start theorising about 'breaking', or looking for a cross to bear: the breaking and the cross are inevitably there at the heart of the matter. C. S. Lewis writes:

Love anything, and your heart will certain be wrung and possibly be broken. If you want to make sure of keeping it intact, you must give your heart to no one, not even to an animal ... the alternative to tragedy, or at least to the risk of tragedy, is damnation. The only place outside of heaven where you can be perfectly safe from the dangers and perturbations of love, is hell. (*The Four Loves*)

In truth, you can discern the bread as that which has been broken in two after being graced with thanks in just the same way that you can discern Christ as the one whose heart was broken in two. So the Body of Christ on earth (the Church) is best discerned as the body of those broken and reformed: 'not many mighty, not many noble, not many wise after the flesh are called' (1 Corinthians 1:26). As E. S. Abbott has said, the question in every age is the same: 'In what man (and woman) will the Lord find on earth a place for the re-enactment of his life and death—not least the passivities of his life?' (Embertide Address in Westminster Abbey, 1965.) Only in this way will the body be discerned and only in this way do we discover the true identity of the Church.

We may carry this parallelism further. Evangelism and mission will often in fact be seen as questions of interpretation and as questions of interpretation of identity. It is only when we identify and discern the tragedies of men and women that we can begin to help them to discover their own identity and destiny in Christ. 'Why has this terrible thing happened to me?' is no prelude to an academic discussion about suffering when people ask it, but part of a *quest for identity*, for meaning in life. The identity of God's people is rooted in the whole story and history of God's people through Old and New Testaments alike, and perhaps it is not until our own lives echo the cry of Job that we begin indeed to turn to Christ to discover our identity within our vocation to be parts of the Body of Christ. 'Have pity on me, O my friend, for the hand of God has touched me'—the same hand which took the bread and broke it; the same hand which was nailed to a Cross; the same hand which takes us in acceptance, blessing and breaking.

The Church on earth is the visible company of people who have found their destiny as interpreted in that Bread which has been taken, blessed, broken and given. Jesus himself found his own identity in relation to the destiny and identity of the Old Testament and its characters both corporately and individually. The quest of this identity is at the heart of much uneasiness in the Church at the present time in simply trying to respond to the question: What is a Christian? The Christian is not a better person or merely a moral human being, but is rather someone whose identity and destiny is bound up inextricably with the destiny and identity of Christ and with the sacramental representation of that action in the life of the altar. So it can be seen that the ministry of the Church in cases of tragedy, whether it be the story of an individual's life or the crisis of a nation, need be a question neither of patronising nor of sympathising. Rather it is an attempt to point and to interpret and to give identity within that great company of men and women who have either prophetically or retrospectively identified themselves with the one great Servant whose life is best re-enacted in the one great Bread, once taken, blessed, broken and given. For that Bread is the life of the world and is the destiny of men and of nations. In its re-ordering, new cohesion, unity and reconciliation are experienced. 'This is your life: this is my life, and this is what life is all about.'

Ultimately this is what life is all about, from the falling of the seed into the ground, to a woman in travail, to man dying to live. It is what prayer is all about—prayer taking many forms, in different people and places, caught up in the central mystery of the breaking of bread. All departments of theology and not least of spirituality have to learn a new poverty, simplicity and Christo-centric awareness. Indeed the whole Church has suffered and undergone a passion which can only point to new birth and new life if we approach it rightly. And again and again arrogant affirmations of this method of prayer or that school of moral theology crumble into dust leaving us for a moment wondering whether there is any specifically Christian morality or attitude to be discerned. It is at these moments that we need again and again to have the simplicity and expectation of the Virgin Mary who was overcome and overshadowed by the Holy Spirit and knew this moment of death as the moment of the birth of a new creation.

The pattern is always the same if the work of Incarnation is to go forward, if 'vehicles of the eternal charity' are to walk in the world and glory is to rest under our feet.

The charismatic renewal

Moments of death rightly approached and accepted can be moments of new life. Man's need is God's opportunity. For it is at precisely these kinds of moment that Christians of all shades and traditions and in all parts of the world are becoming most conscious of what has been called charismatic renewal or the charismatic movement. Not for the first time when foundations are shaken and forms are reformed, a movement of the Spirit is abroad. But the Spirit is fire and wind and both of those images can be seen to be as destructive as they are constructive. So the New Testament presents us with a paradox: 'Resist not the spirits,' yet equally, 'test the spirits, to see whether they be of God.' In the context of this paradox, the present task of the Church is to receive with thanksgiving whatever particular blessings God has found it necessary to give to his people in such a time of need to strengthen them for relating the Gospel 'with power' to the world at large. So the theological injunction which is laid upon the Church is to assess and test this movement of the Spirit without fear or prejudice, and to see it in the light of the total tradition of Christian spirituality. There are two recent writers who are particularly conscious of this task and indispensable to anyone seeking further guidance. One is Simon Tugwell, in his book *Did you receive the Spirit?* and the other is John B. Taylor in his book entitled *The Go-between God*. The former is a brilliant and illuminating piece of scholarship relating the charismatic movement to discussions of traditional spirituality through the ages. The latter is an almost poetic description of growth in the life of the Spirit, using a refreshing vocabulary and a light and exquisite touch in style. Both are positive and affirmative in their views about the movement of the Spirit in the contemporary Church.

For the truth is that for many dyed-in-the-wool Christians, suffering acutely from hardening of the arteries (the Christian cardiac condition!), this new awareness of, and response to, the Holy Spirit has brought a formal life of faith and Christian practice wonderfully alive. In a word, they have had an encounter with the living God. Frequently, this experience has come into the lives of people deeply wounded by emotional disturbance and break-down, bringing a peace, assurance and power beyond any that they could have conceived. Equally truly, the charismatic renewal has arisen at a moment when the Church itself seems to have abandoned much of its cultic religious practice, almost in despair, in favour of a more clinical and cerebral religion, appealing almost solely to the mind and to the daily activity of applied Christian living. At such a time, the charismatic movement has brought about a healthy 'gut reaction' of the religion of the 'bowels' speaking at a far deeper level than conscious rationality and bringing a release and a joy and a quality of praise and prayer for which we should only give thanks. Furthermore it has brought in its wake a revival of genuine ministries, of healing, prophesy, tongues, and a love and freedom which are authentic and compelling in any attempt to bring others to the knowledge of the living God. At its best, it has brought revival and renewal at a time when the rather self-conscious and self-styled forms of what are often described as renewal were at best leaving many cold and at worst had left communities and parishes renewed out of existence! In the sixties, the apostles of renewal were not without their casualties: and most especially when they forgot the Spirit of God.

Nevertheless, we need to ask what are the dangers for such a Church under the power of the charismatic renewal. First there is always the possibility that some dangerous spirit of division might enter Christendom through sharp polarisation between structured and sacramental churches on the one hand, and more arresting 'Spirit-filled' churches on the other. That subtly misleading phrase 'baptism in the Spirit' has created a dangerous brand of Christianity which Tugwell dubs 'Christianity plus'. Christianity plus is no longer Christianity; yet mystical movements like Pentecostalism, which escape from the central stream of Christianity and run the danger of exclusivism, arise precisely in protest against 'Christianity minus'. In so far as they seek to bring people to an authentic experience of the new life in Christ, and so go beyond a tepid and worldly Christianity that has lost it purpose, they are surely sound and even necessary to the survival of the Church. The task of traditional theology must then be to appraise all growth in prayer and spirituality as God given and, in that sense, as charismatic, and to root any charismatic life back to the fuller life of the Body of Christ. The

Body consists of all who, baptised in God's initiative, grow and develop through life in the Spirit, finding new depth in, yet never adding to, the total gift made once for all in covenant and faith. Whatever made us think that there was any prayer that was not charismatic? All prayer is given and originates in the heart and life of God. St Paul could say, 'It is not you who prays but the Holy Spirit who prays in you.' What made us think there was any ministry which was not charismatic? 'Receive the gift of the Holy Spirit for the work and office of a priest in the Church of God.' The task of theology at the present time is not to suppress the charismatic renewal but rather to test it and to give it its place in the traditional life of Christian spirituality while dissuading any lively spiritually gifted groups merely from hiving off from the Body, mistaking certain gifts and experiences as the only test of the authentic life of the Christian Church.

The danger here, as in the world at large, is the danger of polarisation. If we are not careful we shall end up with a stark contrast between the institutional and structured Church on the one hand with its sacramental life, and the 'Spirit filled' and spontaneous Church on the other. In the present world this polarisation is all too self-evident. There is a strong war abroad between institution and Spirit; between politics and idealism; between the rat-race and the flower power; between the utopias of planners and the natural unpolluted paradise of Jonathan Livingston Seagull!

Bones, blood and breath

But if the Christian will listen again to the basic model of his faith—ie the model of the body—you will find that it is possible to contain within that single model room for both the charismatic and the sacramental; the structured and the spontaneous. For in the end the sacramental needs the charismatic, and the charismatic needs the sacramental. If we take the concept of the body we find there are three components: bones, blood and breath and it is precisely this image which Ezekiel takes in his image of renewal in the Old Testament. There are the bones of the structure, the flesh and blood and the breath of the wind. Their application is fairly obvious except for one qualification. John Taylor writes in *The Go-between God*:

> In common with most animistic analyses of the nature of man, the Old Testament distinguishes between *mepesh*, or life force, and *ruach*, or spirit. This always surprises me—for one might have supposed that the breath which man expires at death was an obvious image of the life force. But in fact tribal peoples generally have associated the life force not with breath, but with blood, and the Hebrews were no exception. *Ruach* is a different kind of power inherent in man, associated not so much with his being alive as with his being a person.

Now this seems to me to be an important clue. For certainly Jesus in his institution of the sacrament of the Eucharist was seeing the gift of his life and identity as associated with flesh and blood, yet after the Resurrection the apostles had still to wait to receive the Spirit (even in the Johannine account, Jesus breathes on them after the Resurrection, saying, 'Receive ye the Holy Spirit').

So too with the story of the valley of the bones in Ezekiel and the renewal of God's people. Here is a model of full life restored to its flexibility and its power. The bones and the skeleton are basic and important. There is no life without the structure and the skeleton. But then this is given life and form, features and shape in a clothing of flesh and blood. In some senses it is now alive and even a warm body, but still not a living person until the Spirit blows. Is it too much of a stretch of the imagination to use this model as the key to mature spirituality? If we use it, a useful synthesis suggests itself at the present time. We need no longer set structure against spontaneity, or sacramental against charismatic as if these really were opposite poles. All three elements are needed for a full and mature Christian experience: the basic structure, the flesh-and-blood form, and the breath of the Spirit.

The structure without the form and the Spirit is dead and cannot in any sense be said to communicate life or to be alive. If we rely simply today on the structure of the Church and hope to commend Jesus by trimming the sails and cutting the corners of this structure we shall fail hopelessly, and in that sense it is no surprise that many reject the institutional Church. Nevertheless, sacramental and charismatic without the structure will not be able to stand up in the world of time and space. There is no place on earth for a purely spiritual Church. Further, however, the sacramental and sacerdotal systems can be correct and orthodox, specific and as dependable as a covenant must be, but without the breath of personality and relatedness they will be sterile. The same tension is there in the New Testament between the specific person of Christ and the wind which blows where it wills. The truth is that these last two are essentially complementary; the sacramental needs the charismatic and the charismatic needs the sacramental. Both need to live in and animate a structure and verte-brae.

For always it is necessary to test the life of the Spirit, and the test we can look to is best perhaps outlined in St John's first Epistle—that strange marriage of the loving and the stern. John issues a grave warning that all claims to the Spirit must testify to Jesus and, fur-thermore, testify that Jesus 'came in the flesh'. (1 John 3) This is seen as the acid test of the genuine testimony of the Spirit. Paul in effect applies the same test in the continuous passage in 1 Corinthians Chapters 12–14, where he shows that all gifts should be tested against the plumb line of love—the nature of love as revealed in Christ. In that poetic lyrical passage of 1 Corinthians 13, love is earthed in the graces and good manners of cultured life and there is no heady spiritual unreality about the poetry of Paul's picture of true love in action. For gifts—and these are hard words—are no test in themselves of validity. We are warned in St Matthew's Gospel there will be many at the last day who have a convincing record of raising the dead, casting out devils and healing, yet who will be dismissed as unrecognised by Christ. So also after the mission of seventy in St Luke, the disciples are reminded not to rejoice 'because you cast out devils, but rather that your names are written in heaven'. Gifts of the Spirit, as the Father Creator, are no respector of persons but rather, like the rain and the sunshine, 'they fall on the just and the unjust'. Unless the gifts of the Spirit confess Jesus and relate to the specific covenanted life of Christ forming Christ within us in the day-to-day living and loving of the everyday world, they can be dangerous and even diabolical. In such settings and in such seasons as we now live, 'the angel of darkness parades as the angel of light'. It is not enough simply that the gifts of the Spirit should work through us—they must work in us and form Christ within us. The true work of the Holy Spirit is therefore sanctification. The work of God's Holy Spirit is only a random process and he can work through Balaam's ass! Nevertheless Balaam's ass is not beatified! The Church is not so much men and women *through* whom the Holy Spirit is working, but rather men and women *in* whom the Holy Spirit is working. That process is always to one end; to form Christ within us.

Nevertheless, in case this should sound too strong a note of caution, let me remind Christians of the background of our recent history. Behind this recent break-through of the Spirit of God, there was a period of history which was rigid and sterile in a sacramental system for some Christians, and in a no less rigid and sterile nonconformity opposing it for others. The charismatic renewal is in essence dynamic—a recovery of the thought that God indwells us; that our bodies are his temples; that our works are his fruits; that we all have gifts latent within us, and that as his Body—Christians in fellowship—we are intended to be Christ walking the earth. None of this is novel and none of it is redundant; on any showing, it must be near the heart of the matter. In its light, we can look back at those strange and formal watertight systems of only yesterday which had all too often become religions in themselves, neither pointing to the Father who made us, nor invoking the indwelling Spirit to transform us and to bring light and life to the world. Surely the Church had become largely a cult of the second Person of the Trinity, pointing men to itself—the Body—almost as an end. We can return again then to our triune model recognising that there are three parts in the fullness of the life of the Body of Christ. Perhaps it is no pretension to extend this model to the three-fold model of the three Persons of the Blessed Trinity. The religion of belief in a God whom no man has seen needs the particularity of the Incarnation if its worst anthropomorphisms are to be corrected. The Fatherhood and the transcendence of God the Father demand a particularity and enfleshment of revelation in the Son. But equally, both alike need the Spirit to hold these two together and to bring all alike within their influence and single gaze. 'Our God is not static, an unchanging one—such as philosophy knows of; he is Trinity.' writes Simon Tugwell.

> He is Father, source of all being and beauty and love, origin of all things; he is Son, eternal will of the Father, in whom all things were made; he is Spirit, the gift given to men, whose name is Gift, poured out and distributed so that his very unity seems at stake, unless we 'preserve it' (Ephesians 4:3).

The Spirit yearns in us for the recapitulation of all things in Christ, when the Kingdom will be finally submitted to the Father and God will be all in all. 'That is our God,' concludes Tugwell, 'and our prayer is part of the dynamism which is his truth and his life' (*Did you receive the spirit?*).

So bones and breath are not two alternatives on opposite sides of a world of difference. Each is related through the flesh and blood which gives character and features to the otherwise faceless structure. But if that body is to stand up and walk about and relate to the world at large it needs bones, blood and breath, drawing together in new relationships all kinds of otherwise unrelated people. Such is the necessary presupposition of any new mission of the Church in the world; and could it be that it is precisely for such a mission that the Church is now being prepared in this charismatic renewal? Such a mission will inevitably bring, however, a confrontation with the world and it could be that this period of infused prayer, illumination and warmth in the Spirit which we like to call the charismatic renewal is a kind of corporate transfiguration of the whole Church in preparation for a further 'exodus' of suffering. There is much in theology and history which would underwrite such a comment and such a conclusion. Be that as it may, I cannot see that a 'religious world' as exemplified in the present spiritual and psychic cults, in every modern flight from reason, will in the end be a more friendly companion to a truly Christian witness to the living God than it was in its more immediate history as represented by say Shaw or Wells. In fact religious wars are the bloodiest of all, and there is much to suggest that there will be many who may use the cult of religion for the banners of war in the seventies. One thing is certain, that to secularist and religionist alike the religion of the Blessed Trinity infused by the life and warmth of the Holy Spirit and incarnate in the person of Christ in the particularities of history and in flesh and blood, will constitute a severe challenge and even a positive threat as long as both these present trends of secularism and religionism are seeking to avoid an encounter with the living God. If that is the battle which lies ahead of us we shall need to be equipped for it and the charismatic renewal will be an important prelude to such a confrontation.

At all events, the only task worth giving our life to is the renewal of the institution. Any renewal which seeks to by-pass the institution or the history with which it is laden from the past, will run away into the sands of subjectivism and enthusiasm—and we have been that way many times before! For the parable is the fairy tale of our childhood: 'Beauty and the Beast'. The Church, as institution and as the Spirit-filled Body (and on earth, these are inseparable) is the 'Beast'. There is much in it that attracts and much that repels us. Yet the miracle is the same as the magic moment in the fairy story: embrace the beast, and it becomes a Prince Charming. For only so does God in Christ approach us in all our wretched humanity. He sees in us much that attracts him and much that repels him, but if he is to turn the beast of our self-centred passions into princes and sons of everlasting light he must embrace us. That is the Cross. Shall we in our turn be so élitist and so aesthetic as to refuse to turn to his Body now clothed on earth still in the sinful humanity of which we are a part and refuse to embrace it—albeit also from a cross? For only so will the beast become for us a prince—the Church of our first love, glory with clay on its feet on earth, glory for all earth in heaven.

Pastoral reflections and applications for today

A bishop experiences on a large scale what very few clergy experience—a wide diversity of Christian worship from different traditions, different on practically every Sunday of the year. Sadly, I have to reflect—and for the first time in my life I am compelled to say it—that the worship of our churches lacks authenticity. There are many hurdles which people have to cross before they would even enter a church today, but suppose that, for a variety of reasons, people have crossed those hurdles and find themselves in the ordinary worship of the local parish church. What will they find? I doubt very much that they will find in many cases *authentic* Christian worship: worship which means what it says and says what it means, and which in actions—which speak far louder than words—proclaims and sets forth the Gospel experience in a manner which is arresting for all our senses. Again and again the manner is a whole set of mannerisms: it is bad theatre when it is intended to be theatre, and self-conscious when it is rightly intended to be informal: It lacks the numinous, and most of the time it is trying to be what it is not—cathedral worship when there are only probably twenty-eight people in church.

The worship in the Church today so often misses the point at every point. This has nothing whatever to do with the particular rite that is used. There are churches where 1662 has the sense of renewed worship and authenticity and yet where Series 3 is rigid and unreformed to the point of resembling antiquarianism. It is not necessarily anything to do with the building—again you can go to a modern building which seems to perpetuate every imaginable shibboleth of the past, and an old building on the other hand in which there is an authenticity and freedom, a spontaneity in the worship which is compelling and arresting.

The mark of authentic worship is that it is an appropriate occasion, appropriately expressed. If it is a gathering of young people at a camp in a barn, the challenge is to find an expression of worship appropriate to what is evidently possible. If it is a vast crowd in a huge cathedral it is equally appropriately tailored. So often much that passes for worship is neither one thing nor the other and is the worst combination of both.

The truth is that the liturgical movement cannot in itself bring about renewal. It is not simply a question of updating the rite or moving the furniture around. The liturgy is an outward and visible demonstration of an inward reality and conviction. In other words, spirituality and liturgy must go together, and only when each feeds the other and is complementary to the other is there any real spiritual awakening in the parish or in the life of the local church.

1 *At least three dimensions*   In the story of the evolution of God's people in the Old Testament we can trace at least three dimensions of their worship: The temple, the synagogue and the home. The experience of the temple enshrined for many centuries the sense of the *mysterium tremendum*—God for his own sake—wholly other, transcendent and beyond all our images. From the Exile onwards, however, the Jewish people had to learn that most painful lesson of a spirituality without a temple until it was rebuilt again and before its final destruction in A.D. 70. In this period Jewish spirituality put a strong emphasis on the synagogue as the local gathering, and as being the main expression of its corporate life and its spirituality. But underpinning both these was the spirituality of the home, where the father of the family led his family in worship and prayer and in the various ceremonies of the Passover.

Now although it is dangerous to draw strict parallels between these three dimensions and their equivalent today—because there is not really such a strict parallel theologically—the Church has much to learn from these various emphases in Jewish spirituality: the cathedral, the local church and the house group.

Of course we need to use our cathedrals as great buildings for expressing a worship which speaks in large terms of all that we might associate with the temple. Cathedrals and shrines most definitely have their place and only a false spiritualising would pretend that the Church does not need buildings of any kind. What we do not need, however, is the multiplication of cathedrals or their equivalent. It is good as a diocesan place of pilgrimage to go up to the great Christian cathedral and to experience that worship on a great scale which speaks of the world-wide Church and the transcendence of God.

But you cannot live or grow only at that level. The local unit—the parish unit—should much less resemble the temple and much more the synagogue—a small gathering of fifty or sixty people, with the worship, in everything from the music to the externals, appropriately tailored to express that occasion. And underpinning all this there must be the small house-group, informal but never trivial, local and yet expressing all that is best in such a group of such a size, in such a place and at such a time. This does not necessarily have to be always expressed eucharistically, but can include prayers and intercession, silence, Bible reading and Bible study, discussion or seminar. It can take place around a table after a meal not because the meal is an apology for a Eucharist but because there is a quality of fellowship experienced in a common meal which is as valid as the Eucharist, precisely because it is not the Eucharist. Grace before and after meals is the habitual reminder of this reality.

All these three dimensions can be authentic worship; we do not need to play at cathedrals all the time. The organ is not necessarily the best instrument to accompany the singing of all psalms and spiritual songs nor is it necessary always to have our best silver out or to put the best clothes on! Many postures and mannerisms appropriate to a large building are redundant in smaller buildings and in smaller occasions. Sometimes the simple sign, such as a candle being lit or the exchange of the kiss of peace, will assume a significance and meaning way beyond what could ever have been experienced or made possible in a larger and more formal setting. Formal large-scale worship on Sundays and the Great Days, which is undergirded by these other dimensions has about it the ring of truth and authenticity and rescues the informal from the tyranny of mere informality but equally rescues the formal from what is sham and unreal.

2 'At all times and in all places'   But the norm for God's people is worship 'at all times and in all places'. In practice, however, it is generally only at rather set (and traditional) times and in one place (frequently the least convenient or appropriate). The 'parish-and-people movement' made strides in focusing the main service of the Sunday in the morning, and such a service was usually to be the Eucharist. This is good as far as it goes; unfortunately it does not go far enough. In many ways such a movement was certainly gain in the life of the Church, but it has led to less fortunate side-effects. It has tended to reduce the corporate expression of the life of God's people to being exclusively one of eucharistic occasions: no Bible service, and a reduced reading of the Old Testament and singing of the psalms. Furthermore—and this is much more serious—is the concentration of the Eucharist of the day into one main service. In the ordinary parish it is either nine-thirty (or so) or it is nothing. One time for Mass on Sunday is not the catholic Church. It is in fact the Church of what I have sometimes called—or used to call when you could afford it—'roast-beef-and-Yorkshire-pudding-Christians'! It

is all very well to have one main celebration on the Lord's Day at 9.30am (or so) that will cater quite well for those who go to bed not too late on Saturday evening and get up not too late on Sunday morning. They go to church and then come home to roast beef and Yorkshire pudding! But there are all kinds of people who for all kinds of reasons—good and bad—simply do not go to bed on Saturday night and for whom a Sunday morning religion is just not possible. The Roman Catholic Communion has rightly become flexible about what counts as fulfilling the Sunday obligation, by making Saturday evening Communion possible. In practice Sunday is the most relaxed and free day for most clergy, and surely now the time has come to be much more flexible the other side of the parish-and-people-movement and to begin to fulfil the rule: 'at all times'.

3 *Flexibility*   The great break-through of the liturgical movement, subsequent upon the discovery of the canons of Hippolytus at the end of the nineteenth century, has been the agreement amongst scholars of all traditions on the shape and structure of the liturgy. If Anglo-Catholics in the twenties and thirties could have forseen that, within half a century, Anglicans of all persuasions would be using a liturgy which was structured in uniformity with the whole of the rest of the Christian world and furthermore that such a liturgy would have an unbroken Canon, they would have felt that the Church of England would have exceeded their wildest hopes. This is in fact what has happened.

But such a structural uniformity should give a greater verbal flexibility. It should make orders of service and prayer books redundant. God's people cannot pray the liturgy with bits of paper in their hands or worse still with prayer books and page numbers. So long as we know where we are and what we are doing, the words are secondary. What a pity when the Christian world is becoming more flexible, the Church of England has decided to close the books as it were and produce a prayer book.

If only at this moment Anglican bishops would follow the possibility that the liturgical movement has opened up, by authorising the use of any Canon from any of the churches of the World Council of

Churches and the Roman Catholic Communion, I think this would do more than anything else to bring about an environment of unity. It would teach God's people that liturgy is action, not merely words, and that words are there to help God's people to express their full life in Christ corporately. Furthermore, while we are on this particular subject of unity through the liturgy, is it not possible for all English-speaking Christians to use the same lectionary for the Eucharist? As the Roman Catholic Communion have by far the largest eucharistic attendances in the Western world, could we not adopt their daily lectionary? What a marvellous thing it would be if Christians of all persuasions were reading the scriptures together every day. The common word of God might do more than anything else to create a common people of God.

In all this, flexibility across the traditions is crucial. Extended Eucharists should be much more the norm, and in many places instead of a 'service' advertised at 11.00am on Sunday morning, how refreshing it would be if then—or on a weekday evening—Christians met together for 'apostolic doctrine, fellowship, the breaking of bread and prayers' in some permutation of that catholic formula. If only the agenda for a Tuesday morning or a weekday evening could be something like: a Bible study, discussion group, a prayer meeting, a time for confession, absolution and healing, then the breaking of bread (the eucharistic Canon) followed by a meal together. As a bishop I now sometimes spend a whole evening in a parish for what I like to call a 'Troas' evening (see Acts 20:7–12). It begins with a meal about 6.30pm, and then I take some theme from scripture and study and expound it. Then there are discussion groups. This is followed by a time of prayer and intercession, confession and healing. About 9.15pm or so we begin the Canon of a simple Eucharist where we are sitting in the church hall, and conclude at about 10.00pm. It is in this way that God's people can be fed and built up in the life of Christ; and such a way of conducting an evening leaves room for both the structure and for spontaneity: the sacramental and the charismatic: the head and the heart. It is precisely because we have an agreed structure that we can be more flexible and more spontaneous. For the Church at its richest and fullest contains both aspects of this life and holds them in a holy tension. It is so sad that so many Christians and their pastors hold back from the possibilities that God is offering to us for a richer life of prayer and faith through a new flexibility and spontaneity, yet all the time within the structure, and drawing from the strength of what is given and what is sacramental.

6. RENEWAL AND UNITY

Two cheers for ecumenism

What has happened to the ecumenical movement? The week of Prayer for Christian Unity is in danger of becoming a little like the Cenotaph Service—an embarrassing reminder of what we should be remembering! It is true, as Cardinal Suenens helpfully points out, that the ecumenical movement is a little like the taking off of an aircraft: a lot of noise and commotion at the beginning and then, when it is really airborne and moving, nothing very much seems to be happening and yet at such a time it is equally part of the journey, indeed it is the time when we are travelling faster and covering most of the journey.

It is a helpful analogy because it shows how there are different phases to a movement and that the most important times are not necessarily those which are the most spectacular, most obvious or make the most noise. Pressing the analogy further it might be helpful to trace the main chapters in the history of the movement towards unity, if only to remind ourselves of how far we have travelled and where we are in the journey.

As the thaw of three hundred years or so began at the close of the 19th century and in the opening years of this century, the first and most important exercise for Christians of different traditions was to come together, to meet together, to talk together and to pray together. After all, much of our alienation from one another rested upon images of one another which were largely caricatures drawn by historical memories and perversions. In many ways I would dub this chapter with the general title of the 'Abbé Coutourier chapter'. It was largely his work which emphasised the need to seek all opportunities of meeting between Christians, and it was largely as a result of his inspiration that the Week of Prayer for Christian Unity was begun. Sadly, the Week of Prayer for Christian Unity was largely dominated by talking—platforms of eminent Christian leaders, responding to endless questions and tending to wear their own cap rather more correctly than usual.

However it was an important chapter. In England it was conspicuously the chapter of Bishop Bell of Chichester who by his endless travels and conferences brought together Christians of Churches which had not even met for several hundred years. Christians at last were meeting and beginning to tear down the images of history and looking into one anothers' faces. At last we recognised behind the images and masks the faces of fellow-Christians regardless of their labels. Communication and the media were all a help in this chapter, which culminated with the visit of the Archbishop of Canterbury to see the Pope in 1960, rolling back the shutters of history and breaking the silence of three hundred and fifty years.

However, it was a long time before Churches of the Reformation and the Roman Catholic Church were able even to pray together and I remember clearly how very bold it seemed even in the 1950s to ask a Roman Catholic if we might say the Lord's prayer together. We have travelled a long way since those cautious days and for that we need to give thanks.

The second chapter was what I have sometimes called 'jigsaw ecumenism'. That is to say, the determination to put together pieces of the ecumenical jigsaw which were largely the accidents of history and to make possible as much unity as human effort and the drawing-board could possibly achieve. It was largely the ecumenism of schemes, and helped enormously to clear the ground and to prepare the way for the true work of the Holy Spirit.

Many people felt that the Anglican-Methodist scheme was validly part of that process and perhaps in 1969 when it first came before the

General Synod it was. Yet, I personally felt by 1972—and I am even more convinced with hindsight—that we had moved from that second chapter in the history of ecumenism to a third and more important chapter. In many ways it is a more subtle and difficult chapter to assess and respond to creatively. It is significant that the then Archbishop of Canterbury (Dr Ramsey) concluding the debate in General Synod on the scheme in 1972 said—kindly making reference to a pamphlet which I had circulated to my fellow-members of the Synod—that perhaps 'renewal had overtaken unity'.

I am convinced that this diagnosis was searching and accurate. The process of renewal, conspicuously but by no means exclusively in the charismatic renewal, was becoming evident at the dawn of the seventies and was restyling, reforming and defrosting the large institutional blocks of the Church. The thaw at last was here and if we were lumbered with re-shuffling the Christian Churches only according to historical and institutional blocks, we might actually hinder the process both of unity and renewal. For the dividing lines have moved and changed. The divisions are along different strata and I am certain that a vast legal and institutional scheme, such as was envisaged in the Anglican-Methodist scheme, would have been a lawyers' field-day but would have slowed down and might even have made impossible larger and much more far-reaching movements of renewal towards unity.

Some present cautions

Of course what I am saying comes hardest to the bureaucratic professional ecumenists whose appointments are specifically made to work for unity. It is not easy if you work in an office, spend time on boards and committees and are perpetually asked to speak about ecumenism for you to see the wood for the trees. Unity becomes an end in itself to such a bureaucracy, and before long ecumenism is pursued on a quasi-parliamentary assembly basis—just at a time when many are beginning to see just how unrepresentative and inflexible most parliamentary assemblies have really become.

The Ten Propositions are largely the product of such a mentality and in many ways serve to emphasise just the points that I have been trying to make. Proposition Six, of the Ten Propositions, with its call for the mutual recognition of ministries across the Churches, could actually serve to endorse clericalism and suppress variety in ministry at just that moment in history when we are being led to recognise a real diversity in ministry and to realise that the apostolic ordained ministry is not the last word on the ministries of Christ's catholic Church. Put in a more direct way: I am perfectly prepared to recognise the validity of the ministry of my URC minister as a ministry which is essential in the full Church and which has been lacking in ours. I am not prepared to pretend, however, that his ministry is the same as Catholic Orders and I will certainly not insult him by pretending that they are a second-best variety. His ministry is something in its own right, richly blessed by God and without which the full Church will be lacking and lame. Yes, I want mutual recognition of ministries precisely because they are different. The plenitude of ministry in the Church has been impoverished and limited for far too long—limited in the Anglican tradition to the ordained apostolic ministry almost exclusively.

Some riches are waiting for us if we are honest and open to what the Spirit is saying in all the Churches. Père Congar catches this vision best, when he reminds us that no Church today contains the plenitude of the Church and that we should all press forward to a point of convergence beyond where any of the Churches are at the present time—a convergence which will be a richness and a plenitude making sense of the importance and validity of our past traditions. I have experienced to my cost that when you are driving round Hyde Park Corner, the fatal thing is to look over your shoulder or behind—it is better to press forward to where you are going, giving clear indications and not too many double-minded hesitations! This is not the moment in history for too much stopping to try to keep up with one another but rather for pressing forward for that fullness of life in Christ which is being prepared for us by the Holy Spirit and to which all the Churches need to reach out in faith. Yes, I profoundly believe that renewal is overtaking our schemes of unity and that we have entered a third chapter. We must be careful not to hinder that renewal by holding on to a former chapter in our development and persisting with schemes which no longer reflect where the life of the Churches is really to be found.

Some hard words

However if we really mean business in the end about unity, it is terribly important for the Churches of the Reformation to face some hard facts and some brutal statistics. First we need to get a kind of world-view. This is important because travel and communication in the last fifty years mean that national Churches are no longer seriously worth considering as an entity in themselves. It is as absurd as any form of parochialism when people travel and work and marry and cross continents and when by the end of this century the Pope will be within one hour's travelling distance of the Archbishop of Canterbury.

So let us take a look at the Christian world-scene. For every hundred people in the world, forty are nominally Christians and sixty are not Christians. Of these forty the break-down is as follows:

20 Roman Catholics
10 Orthodox Churches of the East
10 Churches of the Reformation

Of the ten which are Churches of the Reformation the breakdown is:

3 Lutheran
2 Calvinist and Presbyterian
2 Baptist
1 Methodist
1 Anglican
1 Other Churches

Now that picture should put Anglicans especially in their place! Furthermore it should show us that any unity which is not just playing at some ecclesiastical form of the British Empire or the Commonwealth must take seriously the place of the Roman Catholic Church and not least the Roman Catholic Church since Vatican II. In other words, Pan-Protestantism is just burying one's head in the sand. Of course it is easy to pursue Pan-Protestantism for all kinds of reasons, and not least historical. But an analysis of the English religious climate alone demands that we are courageous enough to see what God has done and is doing in the Churches and to respond bravely to that challenge even if it means swallowing many of our words of the past, and utterances which were made with such confidence at the Reformation.

In fact, it does not mean swallowing so many of our Reformation utterances as we might suppose. After all, at the Reformation, the Church of England did not claim to be setting up another catholic Church, but rather to be the catholic Church, reformed, scriptural and vernacular. For the moment, the Roman Catholic Church withdrew from that challenge. However, rather like in the parable in the New Testament of the two sons who were asked by their father to labour in the vineyard: one said he would and did not do so; one said he would not and did. Which did his father's will?

Anglicans said that they would reform and be the catholic reformed scriptural and vernacular Church in England. The Roman Catholic Church said that it would not. But today—since Vatican II—where is the reformed, scriptural, vernacular catholic Church in England? I am not so certain that it is not more conspicuously focused in Victoria Street, London, and that from the point of view of the media, and even from the point of view of the man in the street, the leading Christian presence in England is just as conspicuous at Westminster as at Canterbury. 'There is a tide in the affairs of men', and it is important to read the signs of the times and to respond accordingly. How do I register unity, *now*? There is no way forward for strengthening the Christian presence through unity in England today which ignores the Roman Catholic Church. Of course it is much easier to make a non-sacramental alliance with other Churches and other Christian bodies, but if we are to be true to our Reformation charter then the unity for which we must really seek is a unity between the Anglican Church and the Roman Catholic Church. Bonhoeffer speaks of 'cheap grace' and 'costly grace'. It would not be a bad parallel to speak of 'cheap' and 'costly' ecumenism. It is much easier to speak with my nonconformist brethren about a parity of ministries and to evade the theological issues about the distinctive qualities of the ordained priesthood of the apostolic Church. It is much more difficult to turn to our Roman Catholic brethren and to have a costly discussion about the precise meaning and nature of that priesthood, its distinctive character and its peculiar responsibilities within the total life of the whole Church. The statistics for the United Kingdom are equally worth examination for it is not difficult to see how once again the statistics show that the important blocks of Christians numerically are still undoubtedly the Church of England and the Roman Catholic Church.

The ten largest Churches
By size of 1975 adult membership

1	Church of England	1,862,000
2	Roman Catholic: England and Wales	1,790,980
3	Church of Scotland	1,041,772
4	Methodist Church in Great Britain	541,518
5	Roman Catholic: Scotland	309,000
6	Roman Catholic: Ireland	305,000
7	Presbyterian Church in Ireland	271,316
8	Church of Ireland	176,000
9	United Reformed Church	174,611
10	Baptist Churches in England	155,494

The first three Churches account for more than half the total adult membership of the Christian Churches, and the first seven for more than three-quarters.

These figures are even more astounding when we remember that in 1900 the Roman Catholic Church would scarcely have been seriously listed in the Churches of Christian presence in England. Of course, to think simply in terms of the British Isles is a very limited horizon indeed for our discussion, and perhaps we ought to remember the much larger vision of the world Christian presence. Some words of Douglas Brown, the former Religious Affairs Correspondent of the BBC, make some pretty astounding reading:

> My own hunch is that the Roman Catholic Church will turn towards healing completely the schism with the Orthodox. After all, there are no problems over Orders, and few over discipline and doctrine. The Orthodox Churches, with some one hundred and fifty million members united with a Roman Catholic world-wide membership of seven hundred and seventeen million would indeed be a formidable force amounting, if my arithmetic is right, to about a fifth of the present world population.

It is when we begin to see the picture on this kind of scale that we might well rather brutally ask the question, 'Where have all the ecumenists gone?' It is no use ignoring facts and figures and statistics and talking only of a unity across the Protestant and Reformation Churches. Such an exercise, compared with the real challenge of world-wide catholic ecumenism, is as a game of marbles to a game of bowls!

The Three Agreed Statements on the Eucharist, on ministry and authority are steps in the right direction, though it has to be admitted that the arbitrary decision by the Anglican Church to ordain women to the priesthood will completely undermine any work which has been achieved by these Commissions.* Furthermore such a move will totally discredit any pretensions of the Church of England that it is in any sense claiming to be part of the world-wide catholic Churches of the West and East. Such a move will not only set back all recent steps for unity between ourselves and the Roman Catholic and Orthodox Churches but it will show that in essence the Anglican Church does not really take seriously the limitations and disciplines imposed by effective membership of the world-wide catholic Churches.

A Pope for all Christians

For the day must surely come when all Christians are prepared to consider again what an edition of the *Tablet* (13 November 1976) entitled 'A Pope for all Christians'. Of course, it all depends on what you mean by the papacy. Nevertheless in just the same way as episcopacy does not necessarily mean the prelacy of the Middle Ages, or worse still the pretentiousness and pomposity of the Victorian or Edwardian prelate, neither need a 'Pope for all Christians' necessarily mean all the trappings of a mediaeval papacy. A very great part of disunity among Christians were the inevitable repercussions for a Church which had become so deeply involved in political, economic and social systems, that when these in their turn were fractured or re-ordered, the Church inevitably found itself split across similar dividing lines. The relationship of Church and State today is a very different scene, and certainly does not involve squab-

---

* 'It would be a matter of deep concern were the Anglican Communion to proceed further with the ordination of women without taking very seriously the position of the Roman Catholic Church, our brethren of the Orthodox Church and of the Old Catholic Church regarding so momentous a change' (Cardinal Basil Hume to General Synod).

bles over territories, monarchies, or political marriages. Much that motivated the divisions in the past is just dead history, and there is an opportunity for Christians to meet free from the political overtones which Church leaders inevitably carried in their persons in former generations.

For, if we are to avoid that spiritualising about which we have spoken so much in these pages, then the Body of Christ on earth does not have spiritual members but it has visible members—men and women of every race and colour. Similarly the Body of Christ on earth does not have an invisible head or a spiritual head but a visible head. There is a visible head to the Body of Christ in each diocese—the bishop. In what sense should there be on earth a visible headship to the Body of Christ to preserve the unity of the Spirit in the bond of peace and equally to release a true diversity within the Body which is so necessary for a truly world-wide Church.

That is the most important question facing all Christians of all persuasions today. I cannot believe that history has permitted the papacy to survive unless it retains in some sense the potentiality of being such a visible head of the Church on earth. The concept of a Patriarch is crucial to any understanding of world-wide unity.

'That they may all be one'

The nature and character of the unity for which Christians must yearn, work and pray must be nothing less than the unity which exists at the heart of the Godhead. Such a unity is, of course, beyond our comprehension and so the unity of the Church cannot simply be of our devising. 'That they may all be one as we are one' is the prayer of Christ for his Church on the eve of his Passion. The unity for which Christ prays and the sacrifice in which he suffered are inextricably bound together. In many ways the unity of the Church must be elusive. If ecumenism ever becomes simply an end in itself it will be something other than the unity for which Christ prayed and for which he was prepared to suffer.

The other ingredients of renewal which we have outlined in these chapters are part of this process of unity. We must not isolate the quest for unity from the quest for true holiness, a renewed catholicity and a deeper sense of apostolicity. Here we have to confess that we are faced with paradox and seeming contradiction. Unless the Church is holy, it will not be catholic; unless it is apostolic it will fail to be catholic: only when it is all three of these will it be truly one, and that unity like our Redemption is not the result of our good works or our enthusiasms, but rather it is a gift of God. On the other hand if we sit back and do nothing about it at all we shall fall into the trap of quietism and the devil will rejoice. 'Without him we cannot, without us he will not' (Augustine). Here is the balance between the work of nature and the work of grace; our efforts and God's abundant generosity. The renewal of the Churches must be on all fronts: holiness, catholicity, apostolicity and unity. Our vision of the Church and what it can mean and be will expand if we pursue this route until it encompasses a richness of freedom and a diversity which will be beyond our wildest imaginings.

For the prayer of the Church is always the same, 'That we may so pass through things temporal that we finally lose not the things eternal.' It is not an easy time for being a Christian when there is much loss of faith and a growing opposition to Christian commitment. Pascal writes, 'It is a happy time for the Church when she is sustained by nothing other than God.' That is the only sustenance we need—neither popular acclaim nor worldly success, but the ultimate approbation of God himself. Yet equally this pilgrimage of faith, if it is to be a pilgrimage of growth and maturity, cannot possibly be made in fragmented isolation either from my fellow contemporary Christians or my spiritual ancestors and predecessors. Anything less than a catholic commitment which transcends all barriers of time and space will always run the risk of terminating in a side turning or a cul-de-sac; the winds of history make a cruel and fickle partner, splendid for a quick affair but devastating for those who are looking for more long-term commitment—a commitment for eternity.

For in the end we must be one if we are to enter into our Christian inheritance by sharing in the life of God himself—three Persons and One God. In so far as the thrust of his great love for us has passed through the environment of our history, it must inevitably be broken and fragmented and accompanied by much bloodshed. But in so far as we are also returning through history to the source of that apostolic life in eternity and to rest in God, we must also be reunited;

and this will almost certainly also be wrought only the other side of more bloodshed. I cannot believe that there will be any cheap unity in the last days. It will only be through the inevitable and ultimate confrontation with the powers of darkness that Christians will find their final and lasting unity—a unity of the Spirit in the bond of peace. For like the author of our Salvation, if we are to pray the prayer of unity effectively, it will also be accompanied by Passion and sacrifice, once offered for us: now made effective in us.